THE ARROGANCE OF THE FRENCH

THE RROGANCE

of the

RENCH

Why They Can't Stand Us—
and Why the Feeling Is Mutual

RICHARD Z. CHESNOFF

SENTINEL

SENTINEL
Published by the Penguin Group
Penguin Group (USA) Inc., 375 Hudson Street, New York, New York 10014, U.S.A. • Penguin Group (Canada), 10 Alcorn Avenue, Toronto, Ontario, Canada M4V 3B2 (a division of Pearson Penguin Canada Inc.) • Penguin Books Ltd, 80 Strand, London WC2R 0RL, England • Penguin Ireland, 25 St. Stephen's Green, Dublin 2, Ireland (a division of Penguin Books Ltd) • Penguin Books Australia Ltd, 250 Camberwell Road, Camberwell, Victoria 3124, Australia (a division of Pearson Australia Group Pty Ltd) • Penguin Books India Pvt Ltd, 11 Community Centre, Panchsheel Park, New Delhi – 110 017, India • Penguin Group (NZ), Cnr Airborne and Rosedale Roads, Albany, Auckland 1310, New Zealand (a division of Pearson New Zealand Ltd) • Penguin Books (South Africa) (Pty) Ltd, 24 Sturdee Avenue, Rosebank, Johannesburg 2196, South Africa

Penguin Books Ltd, Registered Offices: 80 Strand, London WC2R 0RL, England

First published in 2005 by Sentinel, a member of Penguin Group (USA) Inc.

10 9 8 7 6 5 4 3 2 1

LIBRARY OF CONGRESS CATALOGING-IN-PUBLICATION DATA

Chesnoff, Richard Z., 1937–
    The arrogance of the French : why they can't stand us and why the feeling is mutual/Richard Z. Chesnoff.
        p. cm.
    Includes index.
    ISBN 1-59523-010-6
    1. National Characteristics, French. 2. National Characteristics, American. 3. France—Foreign public opinion, American. 4. United States—Foreign public opinion, French. 5. France—Foreign relations—United States. 6. United States—Foreign relations—France. 7. Social values—France. 8. Social values—United States. 9. France—Civilization—1945– 10. United States—Civilization—1970– I. Title.

DC34.C443 2005
327.44073—dc22   2004065326

The book is printed on acid-free paper. ∞

Printed in the United States of America

To the memory of my mother,

MARTHA ZELTNER CHESNOFF,

who loved *les chansons*

I have tried to lift France out of the mud. But she will return to her errors and vomitings. I cannot prevent the French from being French.

—*Charles de Gaulle*

MERCIS

Thank you to my editor, Bernadette Malone of Sentinel, whose idea this book was, and to my friend and colleague of nearly forty years Edward Klein, who graciously proposed my name.

A special word of appreciation to Norman Roseman, whose decades in France have given him special understanding of the nation whose problems pain him but which he still loves and believes in. His insights were indispensable as were those of the rest of the members of my Marvelous Midi Mob. *Et merci à la belle Régine.*

CONTENTS

INTRODUCTION

They admire but revile us. They lust for us, then brutally reject us. They love us, they hate us. They envy us, they shower us with arrogance.

In what may well be the most perverse relationship in modern global relations, France has locked its shattered ego in impassioned battle with the very nation that twice saved it from defeat in the twentieth century and yet to which it ironically links the essence of its own political fate.

France's undeclared war on America is no temporary tiff between old friends, no flighty umbrage resulting from a momentary political difference of opinion among allies over the 2003 war in Iraq or over NATO policy. It is a prickly pattern of self-righteous Gallic pouting that began well before America was born, an arrogant spite that has lasted more than two hundred years, and continues to mark the pattern of Euro-American affairs. *Et pourquoi?*

Why indeed! Why would a nation that increasingly revels in Coca-Cola almost as often as it does in wine, which idolizes Hollywood, blue jeans, and the latest in cyber hi-tech view the source of all this as a conglomerate danger? Why would a nation that sends its children to American business schools reject American economic values and denounce everything from globalization to genetically altered vegetables as examples of American hegemony? Why would a General Charles de Gaulle, and those who followed him, thumb their noses at the leaders of the very Atlantic Alliance that saved their republic? Why did the French so treacherously turn their backs on us in our wars against terror, against Libya and Muammar Gadhafi, against the Iraq of Saddam Hussein? Why was that waiter in your Paris restaurant so insultingly arrogant! Why are the French so . . . so damn French?

I've spent fourteen self-flagellating years living and working in France trying to figure out the answers to all those questions. I'm not sure I have them all. But this book is an attempt to provide some—and possibly offer a few suggestions of ways to improve this bizarre, often painful relationship. To do so, I have looked into the hard facts of history, little and well known, as well as into current affairs; I've examined our differences in political philosophy as well as in social mores. I've also attempted to examine French national psychology. (America, the great French singer Yves Montand once told me in an interview, is "the worst kind of beautiful woman: a powerful woman that we desire but feel unworthy of and whom we must therefore degrade.")

I've also drawn on the thoughts of a wide range of figures I've known and interviewed, people from French politics, academia, the arts, and just everyday life. Politicians and professors, artists and actors, financiers and farmers, both those who are

Americana-phobes, and those who mourn the strained relations between our nations; both those whose anti-Americanism is based on specific policy disagreements and those surprisingly many in France who seem to hold a systematic view that the "United States is a danger to all one holds dear."

Obviously, not all agree. Obviously, not everyone in France ignores the fact that France itself increasingly faces a growing litany of dangerous shortcomings, a bubbling cauldron of unsolved problems that threaten its very future.

My loyal housekeeper and friend, Mme Denise Mattano, is one of those. She and her husband, Vincent, among the most decent people I have met in a life of wandering the world, recognize, as do many of my French friends, that no small part of the woes facing the country Denise occasionally refers to as *"la pauvre France"* are self-made problems that can be self-solved.

When I told Denise the subject of my new book, she asked me not to be "too hard on poor France."

I've tried not to be—though, Lord knows, France sometimes seems to deserve it. If I've overstepped the bounds, my apologies to Denise and all my French friends. It isn't for lack of love of *la pauvre France.*

Richard Z. Chesnoff
Le Midi, France
November 2004

THE ARROGANCE OF THE FRENCH

CHAPTER ONE

✦ ✦ ✦

Sixty Million Frenchmen
Can Be Wrong

Next to bicycle races and soccer (or *le foot*, as the French call it) anti-Americanism is arguably Europe's most popular sport. It has been for almost a century, or at least decades—and certainly since we last sent over fleets of our aircraft, ships, arms, as well as several million men and women to liberate the continent.

You name it, and the Europeans are ready to criticize it. What's more, tens of thousands are prepared to come out on the street to shout about and demonstrate against most anything American: be it McDonald's, or our policy on pollution, or our war in Iraq. Even attempts to increase agricultural production through the development of genetically modified grains and vegetables are denounced as an example of America's evil attempt to dominate the world rather than praised as an innovative way of feeding more people. If it weren't so annoying, it would just be boring.

But if America is the country Europeans love to hate, it has to be the ever romantic French who take the continental prize for passion. With a zeal not unlike the kind they invoked to tear down the Bastille, the French are ever ready to attack what they perceive as our "unilateralism" or our "hegemonious ambition," always eager to block us on specific policy moves on the international stage. To the French, we seem evil incarnate. They perceive us as neo-imperialistic, greedy, and ruthlessly competitive—the "hyper-power," as former French foreign minister Hubert Vedrine defined it, a self-serving nation whose riches are acquired at the price of Third World economic destitution and European cultural impoverishment.

In their incessant attacks on us, our culture, our economy, our politics, and our values, the French often seem determined not merely to thwart us but to attack our very soul. It is disdain for America in extremis. When it comes to anti-Americanism, says noted French political thinker Jean-Francois Revel, the difference between France and the rest of Europe is that France "yields the loudest bullhorn on this subject."

This increasingly raucous and almost constant condemnation of American society and values, Revel said in his best-selling but bitterly attacked book *The Anti-American Obsession*, "sweepingly condemns American society as such, branding it as practically the worst association of human beings that history has ever seen."

So very much of this rage seems to be based on sheer ignorance—and/or determination to ignore the facts. As too many Frenchmen see it, says Revel, "America is the 'jungle' par excellence of out-of-control liberalism and 'savage' capitalism, where the rich are always becoming richer . . . while the poor are always becoming poorer and more numerous." Sarcastically, Revel says, "we have it on good authority there is no social security in America, no assistance for the destitute—not the slightest bit of social solidarity."

And in his biting book, Revel attacks the pseudo-intellectuals and political elite whom he says constantly repeat and strengthen the public's acceptance of these "caricatures," the pseudo-intellectuals and political hacks who make a living as members of France's army of America bashers.

Revel, a wartime Resistance hero, and a member of the prestigious Academie Française, was moved to write his book in angry reponse to what he saw as a growing tide of shrill polemic against a nation he very much admires. *The Anti-American Obsession* rose to the top of the French best-seller lists when it was published in 2002. But the distinguished Revel was bitterly attacked and, sadly, his book's effect on French mass and political thinking has been virtually nil.

So why do the French seem to hate us so? Why does a nation that supposedly prides itself on logical thinking and theoretically shares the values of liberty, equality, and fraternity with us go out of its way to "diss" us? Why does a nation that we have helped liberate and save from disaster twice in one century loathe us with such venom? Why does a nation with one of Europe's highest literacy rates show such ignorance? (Come to think of it, according to bookstore sales statistics, most books sold in France are adult comic books.)

Clearly, much of this rabid anti-Americanism is simply an expression of anticapitalism on the part of politicians, intellectuals, and the media—a thought-controlling group in France and the rest of Europe—who, despite all that the continent endured during the twentieth century, remain faithful believers in political philosophies that are at heart unliberal and even totalitarian.

Yet even ideological motivations have emotional limitations. There is definitely something deeper here. There is hatred, and like many hatreds, French disdain for America edges on love, and like all love/hate relationships, it thrives on jealousy.

The French writer and academician Pascal Bruckner agrees. "Envy and jealousy are the two main grounds for the French grudge against America," says Bruckner. "The root is simple—a long time ago, we used to be number one and now that's over. No one in France likes that fact and very few even want to admit that we cannot compete with America. . . . Our biggest problem is that we won't face reality."

But as Bruckner, who is also a popular national radio personality, points out, there is more than just weakness and envy, more than just regret for *les temps perdu*—things past. "It's more of an anti-American passion than a hatred. In any case, we are never indifferent to America. Whatever she does, good or bad, we react—

not like Russia, China or India, or even the rest of Western Europe. . . . America is what reflects our reactions."

Historians agree and point out that, not coincidentally, the moment France ceased to be a great power was about the same moment that America became one. "When France was a great power, America was a nascent power," says Dominique Moisi of France's prestigious Institute for International Relations. "When America became a superpower, we became a middle-size power. And today, now that America is the hyper-power, we are not anywhere near being in the same league . . . that doesn't make us very happy."

One of France's most popular writers, Marek Halter, agrees. "We have been replaced by another empire that is like us but also very different. We are jealous of the successful similarities and detest the differences. We may not like George Bush, but we really want him to love us."

There is another competitive factor: France and America are the only nations in the Western world that sincerely believe that, as a result of their historic development, they offer the rest of the world what they consider to be a universal message of democracy, human rights, and social justice. "The rest of Europe," says Moisi, "doesn't think that way. But we believe that to be French means a certain responsibility to the rest of the world, a responsibility that is inexorably linked to our unique experience: the French Revolution. Americans have the same tradition. And our universalisms are competitive."

The frustrating problem for France, says Moisi, is that "while we may feel the competition for universalism is still going on, we also know that the Americans have already won the battle for power and language."

That may well explain why the French cry "unilateralism" when the United States is forced to act alone because the French-German tandem has failed to take up the task of collective security. It even may explain why the French blindly yell antiglobalization slogans when it is clear that the world's developing countries want more not less access to corporate investment and rich markets.

The fact that France was literally saved by the United States—especially in World War II—has also not done very much to put France at ease. While Britain and the other Allied nations could sincerely celebrate the 1945 defeat of the Nazis as a joint victory, the French could not honestly claim that prize. (Besides, for more than a generation, there were many French of varying degrees of leftist persuasion who remained convinced that it was the Soviet Union that actually won the war.)

In the wake of that war, Charles de Gaulle made indefatigable attempts to paint France as a united nation of resistance fighters. But for all his heroic hubris, the fact remains that France had surrendered to the invading Germans with little fight, and that until Allied forces arrived in France, those among the French who actively resisted the Nazi occupation, or even helped resistance fighters, remained a distinct minority.

It would be more than unfair to say that every Frenchmen actively collaborated with the Nazis. But very, very large numbers did—and enthusiastically. The vast majority of Frenchmen and Frenchwomen were certainly not happy with the German Occupation. But the hard truth is that most of them simply shrugged with classic Gallic gestures, went along with the Nazi presence, and managed as best they could, even if that meant occasionally betraying a neighbor. "You put your conscience aside and tried to survive," was the way one old Parisian once explained it to me.

That kind of unheroic record is not conducive to a meaningful pride in national memory—nor, for that matter, to a balanced sense of gratitude toward the erstwhile Allies who eventually saved France's *derrière.*

In recent years, France's current president, Jacques Chirac, has made some notable public efforts to confront the unpleasantness of his nation's ignoble wartime past, its "inescapable guilt," as he puts it. Even so, to this day, most French still prefer not to talk about their nation's craven behavior during World War II. In fact, until 1974, when an American historian, Columbia University's Robert O. Paxton, revealed the details and the extent of French collaboration in his book *Vichy France,* the French intellectual world all but completely ignored the subject.

So did the French political worlds. In the years after the Liberation of France, some senior Vichy collaborators became confidants of presidents and a few were appointed ministers of government.

Even surviving members of the French Resistance were in broad denial. I was seated once at a Paris dinner party next to a legendary Resistance heroine. I broached the subject of collaboration only to have her insist that "the reports have been exaggerated. Merely a few misguided people collaborated; most French actively supported the Resistance."

Yet a few harsh facts are worth remembering:

- Between 1940 and 1943, more than eighty-five thousand children were born in France and registered as the children of German soldiers.

- The Vichy government not only promulgated a flood of anti-Semitic laws, it eagerly did so even before the Nazis asked them to. Most of the seventy-five thousand French Jews—men, women, and children—deported to Nazi death camps were rounded up and thrown into trucks and freight cars not by Nazi troops but by French policemen, some of whom then greedily looted the confiscated and abandoned property of their hapless countrymen.

- Photographs in Paris taken barely eight weeks before D-Day show tens of thousands of smiling Parisians enthusiastically greeting their collaborationist "president" Philippe Pétain with the facist salute.

- The very last Nazi troops to defend Hitler's Reichstag against the conquering Red Army included devoted members of the Charlemagne Division, a unit of French SS volunteers.

"France," says Moisi, "is the only country in the world besides the United States that derives its national identity largely from its international identity."

The history of French behavior during World War II lent it little support for any sense of national identity. And as France picked up the pieces of its national life in the postwar years, France's intellectual and political leaders—especially those of the left—sought alternative anchors to America.

From the late 1940s, through to the 1990s, and up to the very end of the Cold War, France found itself torn by an almost constant ideological boxing match of savage proportions. In the far left-hand corner was the French Communist Party, for years the second-largest political party in the entire country, and its allies in the non-Communist left. In the right-hand corner: France's pro-Western and anti-Soviet forces.

The Centrist right-wing forces of postwar France had their own misgivings about American influence and power. But the Left, especially the highly influential left-leaning French intelligentsia, rejected them outright. Deeply suspicious of capitalist America, the French Left myopically viewed the Soviet Union as nothing less than the heartland of social equality and progress.

Nothing would sway them otherwise. Critics of Moscow, like Boris Souvarine, a Russian-born French Communist leader who warned early on of the evils of Stalinist rule, were ignored or castigated as anti-Soviet propagandists, or even physically attacked. Throughout the fifties, French personalities from Yves Montand to Jean-Paul Sartre lent their names or marched through the streets of Paris in support of Soviet "peace efforts" and in condemnation of America for everything from nuclear testing to the execution of convicted nuclear spies Julius and Ethel Rosenberg.

Yet not one word was uttered about the systematic repression in the Soviet Union that cost the lives of millions, not one protest about the purges and murders of intellectuals and political opponents, about the starvation and exiling of millions of peasants, about the murderous campaign of Soviet anti-Semitism, about the consistent failures of a system that had proven itself hollow and bare of hope.

Even Nikita Khrushchev's earth-shaking speech before the Twentieth Communist Party Congress of 1958, which detailed so many—but hardly all—of the crimes of the Stalin era, failed to sway the bulk of French intellectuals. "They would not, could not believe that Stalin would have committed such crimes," recalls author Alexandre Adler, who, as a young man, was a member of France's Young Communist League.

Even when the litany of revelations grew, when word of the gulags and the full horrors of Stalinism surfaced, even then many of France's leftist thinkers refused to face hard reality. It was not until the 1980s that the Communist Party of France could finally admit to itself and to its membership that the Soviet Union had not been a "workers' paradise."

Yet that shattering realization did little to assuage the fear, the dislike, and the deep suspicion of America that dwelt in the hearts of the people the French call *les intellectuals*—as if they were a class or profession unto themselves. With their twisted view of the world still seen through a Marxist-Leninist ideological time warp, many on the French Left have stubbornly remained unwilling to accept the new political and social realities, unwilling to admit that just as they had been wrong about the Soviet Union, they had also been wrong about the United States.

For many of these influential figures, America remains a Yankee Godzilla, a witless, awkward cowboy nation that forces its will upon the world, an industrial civilization without any deep culture, a production steamroller driven by a capitalist credo that is as cruel as it is crude. "The verdict delivered against the U.S.," as Revel says, is "as practically the worst association of human beings that history has ever seen."

Here, then, is a concise picture of contemporary America as presented to the French public in a constant stream of frequently vicious articles, books, and televised pontifications: American society is entirely ruled by money. There are no family, moral, religious, civic, cultural, professional values or ethics at play in America other than that bigger is better. American political leaders are in the pockets of either oil companies, the military industrial complex, the agricultural lobby, or the financial manipulators of Wall Street. While a minority lives in lavish luxury, the dominant social reality of the United States is dire poverty. As Revel puts it sardonically: "Hordes of famished indigents are everywhere, while luxurious chauffered limousines with darkened windows glide through the urban wilderness."

When it comes to race relations in America, the French act as though segregation—legal and social—still held sway and the Scottsboro Boys were about to face trial. Notes Adler: "I have to constantly remind people that there are African Americans at the head of some of America's major corporate groups and that George Bush placed two blacks in the political forefront of America."

Nor is there a chapter of American history that is not open to a stream of indignant—and usually exaggerated—French criticism. Assiduously ignoring their own bloody campaigns against North American Indians and colonial African tribes, French wannabe historians harp on accusations that Americans were the New World's great genociders, savagely wiping out the American native-born as we rapaciously swept our way across the continent from east to west. (I once went to see a screening of the 1938 classic *Cimmaron* at an art theater in Paris where the audience actually cheered the Indians.)

"We say we are afraid that America will destroy our culture, our way of life, our independence as well," says Alexandre Adler. "The ignorance is amazing. You would imagine America is a barbarous nation where, for example, capital punishment is universal; no one ever mentions that states like Michigan abolished it forty years ago.

"Ironically," says Adler, "[the values] the United States expresses are the ones France has lost. Belief in God, openness, research, cultural creativity, technological progress, even making a lot of babies . . . France has a feeling it has become a museum and it responds by resenting the fact that America continues to embody the values that we are unable to project. It resembles the loathing of Britain that followed the defeat of Napoleon."

In fact, no small part of French suspicion of America is based on France's own almost genetic fear and loathing of England. Lafayette and Rochambeau may have saved Washington from defeat at Yorktown Heights and brought victory to the young new revolutionary republic. But the ties between America and France have never proven as strong or as secure or even as reflexive as America's ties with the nation that France still considers its ultimate rival and enemy: Britain.

More than two hundred years after the revolution, with our relations to France as frayed as last year's blue-jean cuffs, we still boast of a special "Anglo-American" relationship. Tony Blair became the buddy of a lineage of American presidents, definitely not that of French presidents—especially not Jacques Chirac's. "I have not found a single Englishman who did not feel at home among Americans," the famed French diplomat Talleyrand once said with a sigh, "and not a single Frenchman who did not feel a stranger."

To French minds, that relationship is not only infuriating, it is deemed by many as downright threatening. Call it political paranoia. But in the twists and turns of French historical thinking, Britain has always been "the perfidious Albion," the double-dealing neighbor by the sea that stands ever-poised to plunge a diplomatic, political, or military knife into the Gallic back. (The British view of the "treacherous Frenchies" is not much better. "You must hate a Frenchman as you hate the devil," Lord Nelson once exhorted.)

Even today, with Britain a major part of the European Union and hence conceivably not quite so perfidious, the French still believe in their heart of hearts that *les rosbifs* ("the roast-beefs," as the French call Brits) cannot be trusted to fulfill their European role. London's special relationship with the United States is nothing less than a serious threat to true European integration.

It is also a threat to what has been a major thrust of French foreign policy since the days of General de Gaulle: a concerted attempt to break the Atlantic tie between the two continents in order to enable France to play the commanding role in Europe. To France's absolute horror, British governments since Winston Churchill have systematically rejected that rather pretentious presumption. Indeed, by sustaining the special Anglo-American relationship, and even strengthening it, the French believe that Britain abets American hegemony—American control of the world. It is, if you will, part of an ongoing British plot against La France whose current incarnation is an irritating refusal by Britain to totally commit itself to the European Union.

How else, the French ask, could one explain "the perverse" position Britain took in supporting America in Iraq and in becoming a veritable thorn in the side of European unity?

To add insult to injury, the French continue to witness both the ongoing decline of their precious language's influence in international affairs coupled with the postwar rise of English as the global tongue. "The time was," recalls a veteran diplomat, "if you didn't speak French, you were not considered up to snuff."

Now, ironically, English has become the lingua franca even in the European Parliament at Strasbourg, in eastern France. The resentment is nearing explosive levels. So much so that when Jean-Paul Trichet, the French head of one of the European Union's financial arms, recently began to give his annual report in English, French-speaking members of the audience began to heckle him and then to vacate the forum in protest. Calm was restored only when the hapless gentleman repeated his remarks in French.

To make matters worse, the dreaded *langue des anglais* continues to invade the everyday French lexicon with all the subtle speed of a Patton tank. We Anglophones may not go into serious depression or dangerous rage when we hear the French words *rendezvous* or *tête-à-tête* or *nuance* used in everyday English language conversation. But consider these everyday "French" words: *le weekend, le job, le show business, le supermodel, le upgrade, le coming-out.*

Attempts by French authorities to impose restrictions on the use of English words have fallen flat on their *visage.* When I recently called a well-known Paris hospital to book myself in for an annual outpatient medical examination, I asked in good French for *"un bilan médical."*

"Alors, Monsieur," replied the receptionist. *"Vous voulez un checkup!"*

It's enough to give group conniptions to the Academie

Française—the committee of elders that keeps watch on the French language. But in a nation that watches more American films and TV series than French ones, that now looks to New York for its fashion clues and loves American music and gadgets, a growing use of English seems simply natural. The contradictions in French relations to America are almost as outrageous as the hypocrisy of its policies.

That hypocrisy is nothing less than staggering. The French will rage over endless glasses of wine and tiny cups of dark brew, muttering and moaning about the ignoble way America is destroying the world's atmosphere by its arrogant refusal to commit to the Kyoto Agreement on global pollution. Then, having vented their anger, they will leave and climb into their diesel-fueled cars and mini-vans, vehicles whose exhausts many world experts believe pollute as much and at greater rates than anything Detroit has produced with its catalytic converters.

Almost 70 percent of France's new cars and trucks run on diesel fuel, cheaper than the already exorbitantly expensive French-sold gasoline (about $5.00 a gallon at last fill-up), but considered by many health authorities to be a blight on the atmosphere. Researchers in California, where diesel fuel use is far less than in Europe, have proven that diesel emissions, which can increase asthma attacks, pneumonia, heart disease, and chronic bronchitis, are directly linked to at least seven premature deaths a day. In Europe, it is worse; cleaner technology is being developed, but the European Bulletin of Environment and Health says that diesel-fuel fumes claimed twenty-four thousand English victims in 2002 alone. The French vehicle fleet is the continent's largest diesel-fuel user. Yet little if anything is ever said in the French press or in public about this anomaly. To the contrary, as one French friend told me, "Diesel cars use far less fuel than gasoline cars do, so we pollute less."

When it comes to nuclear power, ecological hypocrisy is just as manifold. French "environmentalists" rant and rave about American nuclear waste but do little to object to the fact that France produces more of its electricity in nuclear plants than any other country in the world—almost 80 percent. What's more, while Belgium, Germany, Spain, and other European nations are determined to close all their nuclear power stations over the next two decades, France has proudly announced plans to build new ones!

The fact is that France has always sanctimoniously believed that it can exempt itself from rules it applies to others. As *Jerusalem Post* columnist Caroline Glick recently wrote: "To this day [France] unilaterally bestows upon itself exclusive privileges. Unlike ordinary nations, it's entitled to meddle in the internal affairs of others."

Who can forget the look on the faces of Canadian officials when Charles de Gaulle proclaimed *"Vive le Quebec Libre!"* during his 1967 visit to Montreal. Or how French president Jacques Chirac and his prissy foreign minister Dominique de Villepin passed moral judgment on American Mideast policy, bitterly condemning "the dangers of unilateralist policies" and blocking attempts at a coalescent United Nations front against Saddam Hussein, while at the same time France unilaterally sent troops into Africa's Côte d'Ivoire to defend its fading interests there.

Nor did the Élysée, always quick to criticize American support for global leaders it touts as dictatorial, see any contradiction in recently hosting Zimbabwe's pariah president Robert Mugabe—defying European Union rulings to boycott him and blocking Parisian traffic so that Mrs. Mugabe and her cronies could carry out their imperial shopping undisturbed.

The history of France's recent role in Black Africa is particularly repugnant. Having reluctantly granted independence to their former colonies less than half a century ago, successive French governments simply created a subempire by weaving a web of neo-colonial rule that enabled them to sustain control over these benighted nations and exploit their resources—often pumping both French private and party coffers full at the same time.

In exchange for a continuous flow of manifold bounties, the French offered protection and support to a long list of African dictators in such countries as Gabon, Togo, and Congo who brutally suppressed and murdered any opposition and looted national treasuries to a degree that made other corrupt world leaders appear magnanimous. Small wonder that one African dictator referred to de Gaulle as "Papa."

Consider just one of France's most important African protégés: the mad, self-annointed "Emperor" of the Central African Republic, the late unlamented Jean-Bédel Bokassa. A former sergeant in the French colonial army, Bokassa seized iron-clad power in 1965, with the implicit authorization of the French government, and wasted no time before he began to bathe in his nation's blood—sometimes literally. In the fourteen years he was the Élysée's boy in the Central African Republic, Bokassa all but drained his country's treasury, transferring vast sums to bank accounts in Switzerland. Untold millions were spent on his 1977 garish coronation, at which, à la Napoleon, he crowned himself emperor and announced he was changing the name of his country to the "Central African Empire."

It was the bloodthirsty rule of this latter-day Caligula that earned him a special place in the despots' Hall of Infamy. Insanely sadistic, Bokassa regularly murdered and frequently dismembered those citizens—and/or their young children—whom he considered opponents or just didn't particularly like. When he was finally overthrown with the help of the French authorities who'd grown weary of all this, his palace refrigerators were reportedly discovered still packed with the bodies of some of his enemies, a number of them carefully stuffed with rice.

Yet none of this malfeasance had prevented the uppity French president Giscard d'Estaing from accepting Bokassa's big-game hunting hospitality (not to mention gifts of diamonds), nor did it prevent France from eventually granting Bokassa and his large family asylum in the land of *liberté, egalité,* and *fraternité* when the evil emperor was forced to flee for his life.

For years, the man behind this pattern of French tolerance for evil dictators was a portly *eminence grise extraordinaire* named Jacques Foccart. A confidant of a long list of Fifth Republic politicians and presidents, Foccart used to list his occupation as "exporter." But his primary export was French influence and his primary import was the political money paid to France and into its political machine by the very nasty pack of African dictators who relied on Foccart's patronage.

The French weakness for power games in Africa was duly passed on to François Mitterrand when he was elected to the presidency in 1981. The Great Socialist gave lip service to the need for "the concrete installation of democracy" in Africa. But it did not keep him from aiding and protecting the French-speaking Hutus who slaughtered the English-speaking Tutsis of Rwanda. The conservative French daily *Le Figaro* once even quoted him as saying that in countries like Rwanda, genocide wasn't really such a big deal.

But no French self-righteous babble irks more than the accusations that our Mideast policy is solely motivated by oil interests. This from the nation (and president) that sold Iraq its first nuclear reactor and in turn received mega-millions in Iraqi oil and industrial deals. Indeed, the full truth of French profiteering from Iraqi oil deals both before and after the UN-imposed embargo in Iraq has yet to surface, as have the full details of alleged contributions to Gaullist electoral funds by Saddam Hussein (once Jacques Chirac's weekend house guest).

If there is one area in which the French can easily compete with America it is in the French predilection for conspiracy theories—one often more perverse than the other. Even now, the French see the CIA's hand in most every major event. The result: a French best-seller whose premise was that the September 11 attack on the Pentagon was an "inside" American operation that had nothing to do with al-Qaeda.

Still, 9/11 had its peculiar impact on Franco-American relations. The Stars and Stripes flew at half mast together with the tricolor from every town hall in France. *"Nous sommes tous les Américains"*—we are all Americans, editorialized *Le Monde,* France's most important newspaper.

"The sentiment was there," says Christine Ockrent, France's best-known woman television commentator. "But only in the immediate aftermath of the tragedy. Then the sentiments cooled down. We just didn't understand the unique and powerful impact 9/11 had on the Americans."

And so it was the war in Iraq that gave the French their greatest opportunity to vent national anger at America. Is it not just possible that it was the shameful vision of France blocking the Anglo-American position at the United Nations that convinced Saddam Hussein that he had nothing to fear from ignoring UN calls to come clean?

Even after the war began, the French continued to fiddle the same dangerous tune. Then foreign minister Dominique de Villepin, who'd diligently led the French diplomatic assault on Washington's policies, told newsmen that he wasn't certain whom he wanted to win. And as we neared the first anniversary of the start of the war to liberate Iraq, the same de Villepin announced to the world that the situation in Iraq was "far worse" than it had been before the war began. Disingenuous at best, de Villepin completely ignored the liberation of Iraq from thirty years of cruel dictatorship, the defeat of a regime that had threatened the entire region, the capture of Saddam Hussein, the first steps toward Iraqi democracy and any hopes for a brighter future—current difficulties notwithstanding. "Here's What America Has Accomplished!"—screamed a headline in a popular French newspaper the day after a savage terrorist attack in Baghdad killed scores of Iraqis.

Like much of Europe, only more so, France continues to vehemently argue that the U.S.-led invasion of Iraq was a cardinal international sin, that the massive deployment of American troops in Iraq and elsewhere in the region is a disaster that has done little but pour gasoline on already flaming anti-Western feelings in the Islamic world.

Yet the French, and their think-alike European partners, have already missed the only intelligent and internationally secure way to resolve the problem: help stabilize Iraq by helping to train and create a meaningful Iraqi security force. Only after the creation of an Iraqi government force that can maintain civil order, that can guard efficiently and forcefully against criminal, terrorist, and die-hard Saddamist forces will a situation exist in Iraq that will strategically facilitate a sensible withdrawal of foreign troops—most specifically the more than one hundred thousand U.S. forces who are there.

Okay, so the French and their Euro-friends have not been prepared to send troops into Iraq. But why have the French basically led the post–Iraq war battle against NATO helping to train such an Iraqi force? There have been vague promises—some suggesting that any NATO training would have to take place in Europe, not in Iraq itself. But as the *Los Angeles Times*'s Ronald Brownstein put it, "That means almost as many Iraqis will probably visit Europe this year for vacation as for training."

Yet if you confront the French and bluntly ask, "Just why do you dislike America so much?," the reply is inevitably an incredulous *mais non!*

"We French love America," insists forty-year-old Philippe Baudoin, a Provence-based art dealer. "You have always been our idol. *'Le Rêve Américain'*—the American dream—has been ours since World War I. But we resent your determination to control the world, to craft it in your own political and economic image—and we dislike your overemphasis on making money at the expense of social benefits. That is the difference between us."

Of such things French myths are made. For the fact is the French would happily attempt to "craft the world" in their own image—as once they tried so earnestly to do—if only France still possessed the power and prestige needed for that trick. And while the ever so elegant French may politely refrain from talking about money as much as we coarse Americans do, financial power has become as important in today's France as it is in America, just more difficult to acquire.

For in the harsh reality of today's France, where almost 10 percent of the population is unemployed, university standards have sharply diminished, crime and poverty grow by shocking leaps and bounds, and French cultural, spiritual, and socially moral omnipotence have long given way to a political blindness that is strangling France's very economic, intellectual, and political future. As Britain's *Daily Telegraph* recently put it: "While Jacques Chirac's France marches across the world stage with its head held high over issues such as Iraq and its relationship with Washington, the reality back at home is that France is becoming an increasingly difficult country to govern, let alone to change."

"Thirty-five-hour workweeks sound wonderful," says French economist Christiane Coudert, "but unless we radically reform we are going broke."

The problem is the French remain enamored of their own sense of social entitlement and fail to see the deluge coming. "We are having a national nervous breakdown," says Alexandre Adler.

Strings of strikes and raucous street protests have done little to improve France's economic future, but do occasionally bring defeat to government candidates, especially in provincial elections, particularly when the government begins to seek economic reform measures. As Britain's *Guardian* put it: "Again and again, [French voters] have voted for the left or the right only to promptly reverse their vote at the following election, making it impossible for long-term programs and policies to be laid down."

It is this failing of France to face up to its own challenges that is a central fabric of France's constant pique with American policy and American success. "We cannot understand," says French academic Alain Duchamps, "why the Americans succeed and have such strength, while we with our moral high ground and intellectual traditions become weaker and weaker and less important to the rest of the world. It frustrates us."

As does the French romance with American culture. "It's schizophrenic," says historian Moisi. "How could a country of such great culture like France fall so madly in love with American culture?"

In some way, says Moisi, "the combination of love and hate is because the U.S. represents a mirror for the French. It is both our dream and our nightmare."

That nightmare is a flat, dreadful global monoculture filled with McDonald's, Starbucks, and other American destroyers of diversity, other American smashers of pure national and folk cultures.

It is a nightmare and an envy that leads to ugly responses to anything American. Take Lance Armstrong, the American cycling star who in 2004 broke all records by winning the venerated Tour de France for the sixth time in a row. Though later greeted politely as a victor in Paris, he had been hounded for weeks before the race by the French press, who wrongly accused him of being involved in doping. What more disgusting manifestation of anti-American feeling could there have been than the sight of French fans jeering Armstrong, holding up drawings of syringes, and even spitting at him as he whizzed past them on the Tour de France route.

Of course, there are those French who are convinced that today's America represents nothing for France to fear. Emmanuel Todd, a young French scholar who should know better, has offered the French a kind of ultimate consolation prize for their current second-rateness. In his roaring best-seller *Après l'Empire*, Todd proffers the ridiculous theory that America is rapidly losing its power, that it is in the last agonizing throes of death, that we are done as a world power, that you don't have to be anti-American because the America that France has known, feared, and loathed doesn't exist anymore. It is dying, maybe even dead.

This America Is Dead theory is a favorite, too, of Dominique de Villepin, one that even now, after he has been dumped as foreign minister, he has been heard to mouth at chic Parisian dinner parties and elegant country lunches.

Thank God, we all still have time to sell our U.S. Treasury notes.

CHAPTER TWO

✢ ✢ ✢

C'est Logique!

WHAT'S ON THE MINDS OF THE FRENCH — REVEALED.

I once lived in the south of France, next to a tiny but messy patch of village land that no one cared for. Being an inveterate green-thumber, I cleaned it up and planted some flowers and tiny shrubs to brighten the neighborhood—an act that, in itself, raised eyebrows on high among my neighbors because, as a local Parisian-born transplant explained, "We are a nation that is suspicious of initiative, that resists change. People in France don't trust anyone who shows initiative. It means they have something up their sleeve, an ulterior motive."

Which may explain in part why the French will rip up someone's cornfields rather than let them experiment with genetically altered vegetables and grains.

Nevertheless, I was encouraged when another neighbor took over a tiny corner of the patch of land and planted his own half-dozen flower plants—petunias and marigolds. Indeed, I felt sublime: My Parisian friend's dire warnings notwithstanding, my Yankee initiative had obviously inspired some neighborly French initiative in someone else.

It also meant that I had someone with whom I could share the upkeep. And so when I weeded, I weeded the entire patch; when I watered, I dutifully watered the entire patch, my flowers and his. Then one day I noticed that when my neighbor watered, he very carefully watered only his six flowers. The line between his and mine was as clearly marked as the 38th parallel, as dry and wet as a line between the sands of the desert and a lushly irrigated orange grove.

I was stupefied.

"Mais c'ést logique," my Parisian friend explained with a knowing smile. "First of all, by planting a few flowers of his own, he is establishing that the patch is not entirely in your control. Secondly, why should he water your plants? What is yours is yours, and what is his is his. *C'ést logique! C'ést tout à fait Cartésien!"*—It's logical! It is totally Cartesian!

And herein lies one of the primary causes of the myopic behavior and cantankerous character of the people of the land they call *La Belle France*—be they overall-clad Midi farmers or overelegantly dressed French diplomats. For as anyone here will tell you, French intellectual life and its educational system traditionally prize a form of thinking that has its source in the writings of one of France's greatest sons—the seventeenth-century founder of modern philosophy: René Descartes.

Though the noble-born Descartes remained a Catholic all his life, he desperately wanted to reform human knowledge on a basis that he thought was safe from skepticism. In other words, he concluded, while one can always doubt experiences, one cannot possibly doubt one's own existence as a thinking being: *cogito, ergo sum*—"I think, therefore I am."

As a result, classic Cartesian thinking prizes logical clarity and a systematic approach to all forms of knowledge. It views clarity and distinction of ideas expressed with lucidity and elegance as the basis of any true act or thought.

So far so good.

Unfortunately, the French decided to zero in on one particularly arrogant aspect of Cartesian thinking and make it nationally sacred forevermore: To be thoroughly original, say the French, one must originate the whole out of oneself. "The things that we conceive very clearly and very distinctly are all true."

Note the "very"—if one sees only clearly and distinctly, it may not be true. But if you see them *very* clearly and *very* distinctly, well, how can you question them? And in any case, whatever you do, don't let somebody else's bothersome opinion or even ugly facts get in the way.

In other words, *au revoir* everyone else!

The net result: a closed system and the core of what we know as French arrogance. Indeed, I think it logical to say that many of France's woes and discomfort in the modern world stem directly from this peculiarly French application of Cartesian thinking.

"Any foreigner who wants to understand the French cannot ignore Cartesianism," says prize-winning French writer Marek Halter.

"When a Frenchman you are negotiating with says '*Cèst normal*,'—he means that what he says or refers to is right and everything that varies from that is wrong," says Paris-based American corporate lawyer Mark Cohen.

"The French believe that for any open issue there is one answer, the right answer. Americans play like football—you move forward, and eventually you get there. The French prefer soccer; getting good position on the field doesn't matter, it's marking the point. They believe that in business the important thing is the result—not being good at discussing the issues."

Cohen gives the following example: "Oral approval is not a commitment in France. An American company would be happy to get a letter of intention. It would mean a step forward, that things were going in the right direction. The French would want the signature—a deal doesn't mean much until the notary has signed it, till it has ribbons and stamps on it and has been registered with the proper government office. That's the way they do things. As far as the French are concerned, the norm is French—everything else is on the periphery, a curiosity."

The system is at its most detrimental in French education.

Thanks to a rigidly centralized educational system under which the French Ministry of Education determines the curriculum throughout the entire country, this uniquely French style of

Cartesian thinking has a firm and crippling hold on the French mind. As a result, wrote the late longtime Paris resident Aram Kevorkian, an American lawyer and a keen observer of the French scene, "generation after generation of French pupils have had their minds 'formed' by the cartesian 'method,' which is a hodge-podge of *a priori* reasoning, formalism, deduction from unproved premises and verbal symmetry."

"Though it's beginning to change," says retired American academic and onetime teacher Norman Roseman, a twenty-five-year veteran of life in France, "French schools—especially *lycées,* high schools—are still full of teachers who believe that their role is to present clearly and coherently exactly what they themselves have learned to generation after generation of students whose task it is to listen, transcribe, and eventually to repeat on examination papers what they have learned from their own teachers. It's a vicious cycle."

So much for creativity and originality; so much for flexibility in international affairs and openness to the policy ideas of others. So much for the ability to focus on more than one thing or one thought at a time. Thanks to M. Descartes, as Lyndon Johnson might have put it, the French can't chew a baguette and *lâcher un vent* (let loose a wind) at the same time.

Kevorkian once described a young French lawyer who came to work for him. "He was brilliant. . . . His only failing was that he was reluctant to have his opinions reviewed by another lawyer. When I asked him if he did not fear making mistakes, his answer was 'Yes, that's why I carefully review my work to make sure there are none.'"

It is this knack for total self-absorption (a characteristic that the British aptly refer to as being "up yourself") that is at the root of so much French arrogance. Notes American philosopher and neurologist Jason Brown, "In contrast to the philosophical problem of appearance and reality, the French have solved it by assuming that appearance *is* reality."

What else could you expect from an educational system that rests so firmly on rote, that rejects innovation, allows rare group effort, has little input from others, and teaches with absolute certainty that France and the French have all the answers—and have had them for some time.

"There are no such things as group projects, group learning, discussions, debates, or exchanges in the French classroom," says Paulina Nivens, a young Franco-American doctoral student who has studied on both sides of the Atlantic. "It's changing somewhat, but most learning in France is still done in solitude, by one's own means. In French universities," says Nivens, who now studies at Vanderbilt University in Nashville, Tennessee, "you have lectures only and then examinations on those lectures. There are no such things as seminars. Worst of all, the opinions of others are of little or no import."

Small wonder then that France appears so absolutely contrary in international forums.

Worse yet, while Descartes wrote in Latin, he placed enormous import on language—one's own language above all the rest. Accordingly, the French educational system has traditionally placed enormous importance on the French language at the expense of other languages and at the expense of the reality of the diminished utility of French in worldly affairs. Instead, what is stressed over and over is the development and importance of the French language in the pages of history. *C'ést logique.* After all, as the café owner in a nearby town once reminded me, it was French, not English or German, that was the language spoken by all the royal ruling families across Europe.

I hastened to remind him that while many of these avid French speakers may still consider themselves royal, for the most part, none are really ruling anymore. More to the point, English is the language now being spoken in international forums.

"Tant pis," he replied. Too bad.

The net result: While there is still some emphasis in elite high schools on the study of Latin with its logical syntax, there is little encouragement most anywhere for French students to learn anything other than the rudiments of other modern languages (which, one can argue, has been the case in the United States as well, but for other reasons). It is, as my old Latin teacher might have said, a *causus solitudinis.*

Cartesian thinking, in fact, has led to an amazingly insular mentality among many French young people. For all their fascination with American culture and love of exotica, few French students emulate their American and other European contemporaries with anything resembling a drive to travel as part of their education. "The saying," says Nivens, "is that 'France has it all—mountains, beaches, forests as well as every possible type of climate for every possible occasion and activity. So why travel elsewhere when you have everything here?'"

This national sense of smug perfection translates into a general lack of interest for other cultures and other modes of life that bordered for a very long time on repudiation. It's beginning to change, but the effect is still there. It has allowed the French to incorporate into every aspect of their life among the lesser nations of the world, a concept that they actually dare to call "the French exception"—in other words, France's divinely granted ability to exclude itself from cultural, economic, and even technological norms and to establish its own peculiarly French ones. One annoying example: While almost all of Europe uses the PAL system of television, the French insist on their own SECAM system, which they share with the former Soviet Union. After all, *c'ést logique.*

Descartes, says Kevorkian, "could not content himself with 'God exists, the Bishop told me so.' But he could get away with 'God exists, because He allowed me to see the light.'"

So generations of French "intellectuals" became modern while clinging to their Divinely inspired tradition. "There is something very touching about the French faith in reason," notes Kevorkian. "It is no accident that in the most fanatic period of the French

Revolution, the Christian deity was replaced by the Goddess of Reason."

But that worship of reason has also led to an almost churlish French obedience to authority. Along with it comes a tolerance for conflicts of interest and a disturbingly myopic view of governmental and corporate corruption.

Some believe—and I tend to agree—that for all their republicanism, the institutions of France are still dominated by clerical-monarchial perceptions. For all its *liberté, égalité, et fraternité,* France adheres to authoritarian values. If the United States is a horizontal society where ethics and standards are set by a consensus of the public, France is a vertical society where rules and regulations come from on high. In prerevolutionary days it came from the king and from the princes of the church; today, law, rules, and decrees come down from the central republican government. Under the rules of the Fifth Republic, the French presidency carries far more executive power than its American counterpart.

That message was made most clear on July 14, 2004. In his annual Bastille Day interview with France's two largest TV channels, President Jacques Chirac was asked about a growing political challenge to him from his young and dynamic then minister of finance Nicolas Sarkozy, or from any other members of his government. "It is I who decide, and they who execute," he announced regally.

"The French may joke at Chirac's occasional regal outbursts," says Norman Roseman, "but they accept his regalian manner.

The monarchial idea was rejected in the eighteenth century, but it still resonates loudly today because it is embedded in the collective psyche."

It was the ultimate expression of what some French analysts call *la monarchie républicaine,* a contradiction of pompous proportion that was enthroned by de Gaulle but artistically fine-tuned by Chirac and his immediate predecessor, François Mitterrand.

I once interviewed Mitterrand together with Mortimer Zuckerman, my editor in chief at *U.S. News & World Report.* We were ushered into a tastefully furnished Élysée conservatory where the imperious leader of French socialism greeted us attired in a *haute couture* version of a black shepherd's jacket—a sort of male rendition of Marie Antoinette attired as Bo-Peep.

Before we began our questions, he motioned to me to approach him.

"You know," he said, "in France the journals always reprint *every* word of a presidential interview."

I explained that we didn't necessarily do it that way in America. I don't think M. le Président de la République was pleased.

True enough, the French directly and democratically elect their president (for a five-year term) and the 577 representatives in their National Assembly (for five-year terms). The 318 members of the Senate are elected by an electoral college for nine years. The members of twenty-two regional councils are directly elected. But the officials who truly control the lives of more then sixty million Frenchmen and Frenchwomen are appointed by the regional councils. I speak of those classic French figures of power, the Prefects, the sort of governors of France's ninety-six districts.

The "Préfecture" is the place you go to register your car, and to get your driving permit, your passport, your identity papers, and just about everything that proves you are alive and kicking. (One old American friend who lived and worked in France for years, and dutifully paid French income and social security taxes, now collects a French social security benefit each month. Once a year, however, he must submit documents to the French embassy in Washington to prove beyond a shadow of a doubt that he's still alive.) It is also the site of the best and the worst in French bureaucracy.

There are without doubt few things more tedious or challenging than a French driving test. But for people who choose to live here, a French driver's license is a must. Without it, as my insurance agent explained, your car is without value. Fortunately, some American states have reciprocal agreements with the French for a sort of even-steven exchange (for example, if you have a valid New York license, you can automatically get a French license in exchange).

The key word here is "some," because for some inexplicable reason these state-nation reciprocal accords are limited to ten—or twelve or thirteen of the good old U.S. of A.—depending at which prefecture you apply.

Fortunately, for me, my old home state of Connecticut was among the lucky ten everyone seems to know about. All I had to do, I was told, was fill out a form, leave two photos, and show my passport, resident's permit, and my Connecticut DMV license along with a certified French translation.

"We will contact you, Monsieur, when your French license is ready. Then you must come here and we confiscate your Connecticut license from you."

"Et pourquoi?" I asked the *fonctionnaire* at the license window.

"*C'ést logique, Monsieur!* How can one person have two driving licenses?"

I tried to appeal to her French perception of savage America. "Yes, Madame, but what do I do if I'm back visiting in the U.S.A. and am driving in some wild, unsophisticated part of the country—say, Texas—and I have to show my license to a Texas Ranger who doesn't understand a word of French?"

"Well, you could apply here for an international license as well. They come in five languages. Surely, he'll understand one of those."

But doesn't that represent a second license?

Ahhh non, Monsieur. That is *tout à fait différent.*

So I applied for both and two months later received a note from the Prefecture instructing me to come to pick up my new driving permits. When I arrived, ready to hand in my Connecticut license, I found that only the pink French license was ready. The gray international license had not yet been drawn up. Okay, said I, I'll come back when they're both ready. Meantime, I'll hold on to my Connecticut permit.

The clerk shrugged.

Some weeks later I received notification that both the international and French licenses were ready. And when I came to the Prefecture, I was ceremonially handed both of them—but for some reason no one asked me to turn over the Connecticut license. So now I have three licenses.

Truth to tell, the way the French drive, the more licenses you have, the better off you may be. I think it was Henry Ford who once said (or at least he should have said), "You can judge a nation by the way it drives." If H.F. actually did utter those words, he probably had France in mind.

Few nations know more or care more about automobiles than the French. They worry about them, talk about them, covet them, wash them, polish them, and frequently love them more than their children and wives . . . even more than their dogs.

But put a Frenchman behind a wheel and his passion for *l'auto* turns to sadomasochistic aggression. He may be behind the wheel of a tiny Citroën, but he might as well be on the Indianapolis Speedway in a Maseratti or manning a superpower Leclerc tank on the road into Timbuctoo—speed is of the essence, and God help anyone who gets in the way. It is a single-minded heartless drive to win.

But why do they drive as if they were wielding AK-47s? What persuades them that their tiny Renault can pass you and the oncoming car at seventy-five miles an hour on a frighteningly narrow, and inexorably winding, country lane? Why is ninety miles an hour not enough on an open highway? Why must it be one hundred? Why is any driver who sticks to speed limits considered a *con* (jerk)? Why is natural aggression as much a necessary tool of driving on French roads as good eyesight and rapid reflexes?

British writer David Hampshire puts it this way: "The personalities of most Frenchmen change the moment they get behind the wheel of a car, when even the most placid person can become an aggressive, impatient and intolerant homicidal maniac with an unshakable conviction in his own immortality."

Hampshire is right. And perversely enough, the most aggressive of the drivers (this based on an informal poll of visiting friends) are not those big deals from Paris in their fancy Mercedes air-conditioned SUVs, but the otherwise docile and slow-moving folks of Midi in their tiny trucks and budget two-door model Citroëns.

I have developed my own theories. One is that Frenchmen are convinced that every time someone succeeds in passing them on the road and/or, God forbid, they fail to pass someone else, they automatically lose one millimeter in length from their manhood.

Well, you might ask, what about female French drivers, who are not much better nor any safer than fellow drivers on any road? Envy?

And who has hasn't driven on a French *autoroute* already amazed that you are more or less legally speeding at the equivalent of ninety miles an hour, only to suddenly gaze into your rearview mirror and discover a hitherto unseen car, its headlights flashing uppers and downers, following so close to your rear bumper that you are convinced it's attached to your car like an automotive version of Siamese twins.

Like speeding on roads and overtaking on narrow curves, tailgating in extremis is a national passion—no matter what the speed, no matter what the traffic, no matter how bad the weather.

Perhaps the ultimate reason why the French reject the very idea that they cannot pass someone on a highway or that, perish the thought, someone else passes them, stems from what may well be a psychotic fear of being humiliated, of being demeaned, or of just being wrong. "Look at the way the French are taught their own language," says Paris psychotherapist Brenda Foguel. "There is only one right way of saying something, therefore it is very easy to be wrong. And because language and concepts are so rigid, the experience of being wrong is especially humiliating. The French experience being wrong as a narcissistic wound rather than just a simple mistake."

Indeed, according to Foguel, it is the very fear of being wrong that unconsciously intensifies the rigidity of what is supposedly right.

The traditional French education system relied heavily on the art of humiliation. There was no coddling of kids in Gaul. It was the old "if you make a mistake, stand in the corner, wear a dunce-*chapeau*, you are a little fool " syndrome—a self-fulfilling prophecy that in this day of somewhat more enlightened young teachers still makes every French child quake in fear of ever being wrong. One result of which is that few French will ever admit to being wrong about *anything*! La Marseilles could be replaced as a national anthem by that old Edith Piaf song, "Je Ne Regrette Rien"—I have no regrets. *"C'ést pas de ma faute"*—it's not my fault—could well serve as a national motto.

Not long ago I crossed a street in a nearby town in order to enter a grocery store. There was a bicycle precariously perched outside. As I neared the door, the shop owner, who was adjusting his awning, inadvertently touched the bike, knocking it down and straight onto my leg.

I wasn't hurt and the shopkeeper did look at me sympathetically as I rubbed my leg and then picked up the bike. But he said nothing.

"At least," I offered, "you could say 'I'm sorry.'"

"Why should I?" he asked with a quizzical look. "It's not my bicycle."

Then there was my French acquaintance in a nearby village who is a motorcycle enthusiast—a love he inherited from his father, who, at eighty-five, still rides his own *moto* whenever his family will allow him.

One day this senior Hell's Angel skidded his motorcyle on the village road and took a terrific spill. Everyone rushed to his side to help—and to make sure he wasn't dead. The first words out of the old man's mouth were *"Ce n'étais pas de ma faute"*—It wasn't my fault.

All of which means that the only way to ensure your continued innocence is to pass guilt on from person to person—like a hot potato of shame. If the plumber makes a mistake, he blames it on the mason, who then blames it on the stone cutter, who then blames it on the carpenter, who then finds some way to blame it on the electrician. Ultimately, however, you are at the tail end of the pecking order. *C'ést de votre faute.* It's your fault.

Consider this strange tale. More than twenty years ago, two old friends in Manila, Tessie and Tito Yulo, presented me with an unexpected gift from their own exquisite collection of Spanish and Philippine colonial antiques: an eighteenth-century figure of St. Joseph with the infant Jesus perched in his arms. Both father and son have faces and hands of carved ivory. Both are dressed in original handsome gold brocade fabric, and there is a gold crown atop Jesus' silken hair and a gold staff in Joseph's hand. Mounted on a handsome polychromed base, the sacred statue stands some twenty-two inches in height.

Years later, when I moved to my Midi village, I decided that though not a Catholic, I would donate the antique statue to the tiny village church as a way of introducing myself and as a gesture of thanks for welcoming me into their local community.

Though 75 percent of the French population is still nominally Catholic, most parishes can no longer afford to support a full-time village priest. Instead, there is a circuit priest who performs Mass in a different village each week, while the day-to-day needs of church maintenance are carried out by a local parishioner.

My neighbor, Mme J., the *diaconesse* (deacon) of the village church, seemed delighted with my gift. "Are you Catholic or Protestant?" she asked me.

"Neither," I said, "I am a Jew."

"Oh well," she said, not missing a beat. "We are all children of God."

The figure of St. Joseph and Jesus was placed atop one of the altars, I purchased an antique glass dome to protect it and a wooden platform for it all to stand upon, and eventually—after asking why I hadn't received one—actually received a hand-written note of thanks on foolscap from the circuit priest whom I was told was about to retire.

"You must make a plaque for your offering with your name and the date you gave it to the church," Mme J. told me.

Three years passed before I ever got around to having the plaque made. I would place it on the base of the statue myself. So I arranged with Mme J. to come to the church just before one of the irregular Sunday Masses and after meeting the new circuit priest, picked up the statue platform and took it home to affix the plaque. When Mass was over, I returned and began to replace the statue atop the platform on the side of the altar.

It was then that the priest approached me and in a decidedly accusatory tone demanded to know: "Who gave you permission to place that figure here, Monsieur?"

Mme J., who was standing nearby, said nothing.

"Father, I'm a little confused," I replied. "This figure was a gift of mine and has been here in the church for more than three years, Mme J. knows all about it, and your predecessor even sent me a note of thanks—"

He was unfazed and cut me off. "This is a church, Monsieur; we have rules and regulations and you cannot do whatever you want."

Not a little shaken by his attitude, I glanced toward Mme J. in anticipation of some backup. None was forthcoming. She remained silent.

Shaken, I managed to say *"Pas de problème, mon père,"* and began to pack up St. Joseph and Jesus. "I'll take it out of the church and back home with me."

"He didn't know it had been there for three years," the hitherto silent Mme J. finally told me in a stage whisper. No "sorry for the misunderstanding," no apology from the now properly informed priest.

"Desolée," I replied as I finished carefully loading my now unwanted gift in a straw basket, and carried it out of the church and back to my home.

To this day, I have heard nothing from either Mme J. or the offensive village priest. I have no idea what the real problem was. But I was left with the distinct feeling that somehow it was and always will be considered *ma faute.*

Not that there isn't a distinct strain of forgiveness in national attitudes—certainly if such charity serves a distinct purpose. The French jettisoned the heads of their king and queen more than two hundred years ago. But they haven't cut themselves off from an abiding and often avid interest in the comings and goings of inconsequential royalty. I mean, what would French mass-media magazines like *Paris Match* do without such internationally important royal personalities as the Grimaldis of Monaco? The two dysfunctional daughters and one questionable son of Prince Rainier and the late Grace Kelly are cover meat for the magazine on an ad nauseum basis—as are stories about the royal progeny of neighboring Spain, Belgium, and the Netherlands. Even the young king of Morocco rates an insider story from time to time.

Still, if you really want to win the week's French circulation war, all you need is a cover picture and some inside, full-page out-of-focus photos that illustrate the newest slop about Princess Stephanie's latest fling with one of her bodyguards or with a traveling circus acrobat. Now there's a surefire seller!

I know, we have our own fixation with Princess "Di" and the surviving British royals . . . but at least they're significant. After all, they speak English!

Of course, the French also share our perversion for pop-star gossip and dribble. Problem is that while we may waste pages of magazine copy and hours of TV time on which Jackson brother or sister has bared his or her breast, and who's doing Ben Affleck, at least there's a new name every once in a while.

The French, those lovers of tradition and classics, seem to focus on the same handful of personalities. The main man in this perennial popularity pack is undoubtedly one of the country's least talented people—an aging Belgian-born rock star named Johnny Halliday who has been wowing the French public with his poor man's Elvis routines for more than forty years. "Johnny," as he is called by everyone who knows or would like to know him, is enormously wealthy and has had an enviable stream of lady loves, all of whom seemed to grow younger as he grew older.

Traditionally, of course, the French have always had a much more tolerant attitude toward sex than we Americans do. Sex and State are certainly considered as sacredly separate as much—if not more—than even Church and State.

The formidable Charles de Gaulle was possibly too frightened of his even more formidable wife, the stern woman everyone called Tante Yvonne, to fool around—or may not have been so inclined. But the general's successors have more than made up for his unflinching fidelity. Georges Pompidou, Valery Giscard d'Estaing, François Mitterrand, and Jacques Chirac were or are all known to have an eye for the ladies, and those who bother to find out such things usually know the names and professions of some rather specific ones.

The late Socialist leader François Mitterrand was arguably among the most active of the long list of presidential philanderers whose peccadilloes have marked the history of French politics during all five of the postrevolutionary republics.

"C'est sa nature," that's the way he is, was the expression. It was accepted. When Mitterrand died after a lengthy bout of prostate cancer, it was in the state-owned apartment of one of his mis-

tresses, Anne Pingeot. While that raised a few eyebrows, no one in France even blinked an eye when Ms. Pingeot and their illegitimate daughter, Mazarine, a young woman whose name and face had only recently become known to the general public, showed up as honored guests at his village funeral. Nor did anyone think it the slightest bit bizarre that Mitterrand's widow, Danielle, and his two sons embraced them both warmly in an almost royal family-in-mourning scene.

"You see what a civilized people we are," a French friend told me in the midst of the Clinton-Monica scandal. "Not like you silly Americans, who think you've had a national tragedy because some young girl pleasured your president in the White House."

Indeed, the only thing that seemed to upset the French, who have an abiding affection for the *charmant* Clinton, was what they considered Bill's horribly bad taste in women. *"Elles ne sont pas très chic ni pas très sexy"*—they're neither especially chic nor very sexy, seemed to be the popular wisdom.

Yet while the French are true to their national image of being open about sex, they remain quite reserved when it comes to the rules of politesse. The owner of the little *boulangerie* where you buy your croissant, or the *petit commerçant* who sells you your daily newspaper will fall all over you with *bon jours* and *mercis* every time you come through the door to make your purchase, but conversation must be limited to niceties. People you have met just once at a dinner party may well kiss you on both cheeks upon meeting you on the street (three times in this region), but it will be sometime, if ever, before you will be allowed to refer to each other with the familiar *tu* as opposed to the more formal *vous*. Ten-year-old boys will formally shake hands with each other as they arrive and leave school, but if you smile and say *bon jour* to someone on the street that you don't know, as is the frequent wont among overly friendly Americans, you will be greeted in return by an icy stare.

The French think they have a special knack for imperiously insulting you without your knowing it. Of course, the classically surly French attitude is generally more transparent than they may realize—and according to one dear French friend is actually intended to be just that. The real talent, my friend said, was to be "polite and insulting at the same time. That's the sophisticated put-down" (see Addendum One).

A few examples: At the urging of friends, I went to dine one evening in a nearby country restaurant that had recently acquired a new chef and a reputation for much improved cuisine. It also had a long-standing reputation for being a little stuffy. But a good meal with friends is a good meal, and off we went.

We were greeted by a slick-haired, mustachioed maître d'hotel in a suit and tie surrounded by five young and nervous-looking waiters and waitresses in formal black—already a threatening sign in the otherwise wonderfully relaxed atmosphere of Midi.

"Vous-avez reservé, Monsieur?" he asked with appropriate snoot.

"Have you reserved?" Like I would come to one of the fanciest restaurants in the region without one!

I gave him the name of the friend who had reserved. "You are eight people?" he asked, still hoping to catch me. To which I replied I had no idea since I hadn't made the reservation. However, I noted, since he or a member of his staff had taken the reservation, he should already know how many we would be.

It was all downhill from there. When the time came to order the wine, M. Le Snoot played the wine steward as well. I wanted to start with a white Lirac, a local wine whose red I knew well but whose white I'd never tasted. There were two on the wine list and I told him I would leave the choice to him.

"Extraordinaire," he said, the sarcasm almost dripping from his lips.

The young waiter who served us was delightful. We never saw the maître d'hotel again. Although he was omnipresent on the dining terrace, he never once bothered to stop at our table to ask whether we were enjoying our meal, or even to say good night and thank you after we'd dropped some $750 for our just-okay meals and the rather good wines and began to head for the door.

It was one of those moments when I became furious enough with this classic type of French impoliteness that I decided to confront it head-on. But I was so ticked, I was afraid my French would fail me.

"Est-ce que vous parlez Anglais, Monsieur," I asked.

"I trrryyy," he replied in his best Charles Boyer accent.

Well, I said, "I think you are extremely impolite and unprofessional. You had eight new clients here tonight and you made no effort to see how they were faring or even to say thank you and good-bye. You are very disagreeable."

He stared at me as though I were a cockroach he'd discovered in his cuisine, said nothing, and turned on what I'm ready to bet were his slightly elevated heels.

All of these indignities can be multiplied tenfold when one chooses, as I have done, to spend most of one's time among the French. For example, my neighbor in the tiny French farming town where I live doesn't like me. In fact, he detests me. Monsieur Trudecul (not his real name, but close enough in spirit) doesn't care for foreigners. As far as he's concerned, *les étrangers ont emmerdé le village*—literally, the foreigners have crapped up the village.

What he means is that wide-eyed outsiders like me have had the gall (no pun intended) to come to this beautiful little hillside town in the Midi—the French equivalent of the Deep South—and then enthusiastically overpay to buy old village houses from bemused villagers who, unlike my neighbor, are willing to take *les étrangers'* dollars, pounds, francs, and euros.

Most of the properties we buy are actually little more than run-down structures, often houses long abandoned to winter rains and summer mistrals and, as a result, sometimes not much more than piles of medieval stone and earth, albeit very romantic piles of medieval stone and earth.

We then hire local craftsmen to help us renovate these super picturesque ruins and, after much expense (triple the estimates) and enormous stress ("But Monsieur, I said I'll come on Tuesday, but I just didn't say which Tuesday"), transform them into what we consider super charming houses and gardens worthy of at least a two-page spread in that chicest of regional French decorating magazines, *Côté Sud.*

In my town, this invasion by foreigners has certainly saved what is known as "The Old Village" from tumbling into total ruin. The houses we "attack," as the French expression goes, generally all end up looking a lot nicer than Monsieur Trudecul's house and garden ever have, do, or will.

Not that Monsieur T. can't afford to do the same or similar. According to local lore, his father had a little money, and during the war, when other farmers were forced to sell land to feed their families, Papa T. managed to buy up significant tracts around town and, according to the best informed sources at the local café, his son is "as rich as Croesus."

What bothers him is the very fact that we have done what we have done—and sin of all sins, we're not from here. That makes him envious and the envy makes him increasingly angry and bitter. So he gets back at us *étrangers* by insulting us, by not responding to our *bon jour,* by causing us problems, by parking his car in a way that makes it hard for anyone else to park, and, when he passes us, by loudly mumbling to himself in that incomprehensible way the French have when they are annoyed with anyone, especially a foreigner.

I tried to make friends. I introduced myself immediately after I bought my six-hundred-year-old ruin. I sent him a bottle of champagne at Christmastime to apologize for all the construction noise. And when he angrily informed me that one of my workers had mistakenly moved an empty planter on the street in front of my house that actually belonged to him, I returned it dutifully planted with new posies and a little fir tree. I even asked his advice on pruning the wild plum trees in my garden. But it was a no-win situation.

Monsieur Trudecul was determined not to like me. For beginners, I was a foreigner, then I was an American, and as if all that weren't bad enough, it probably didn't help that I was a J-E-W. He was, I was told, a fervent supporter of France's extreme right-wing racist demagogue, Jean-Marie Le Pen—a man who once described the Holocaust as nothing but "a detail of history."

I suppose in M. Trudecul's closed mind, it could have been worse. I could have been a Moroccan Muslim with a black wife and ten children.

Of course, not everyone in the village is as hostile as Monsieur T. Many of my fellow villagers occasionally offer a polite hello when I meet them on the street or at the weekly market in the nearby town. Quite a few took the liberty of stopping by to see what I was spending all my money on during the construction period—often amazed that I was installing more than two bathrooms. And a few aged souls still stop by occasionally to chatter away to me about their childhood memories of the days when the village had no paving, no sewers, and one car—possibly because no else in the village will listen to them anymore.

The rest of the foreigners in town—mostly vacation-home owners—hail from Germany, England, Sweden, Switzerland, and other European locales. We occasionally socialize over cool glasses of rosé wine and complain about the villagers. But I am one of the few year-round foreign residents, and in four years here, only one French family has ever so much as invited me into their home for an aperitif. And technically, I have to exclude them; they're not originally from the village, they're Parisian—hardly considered native sons and daughters by the traditionally xenophobic farmers of the Midi. As the local expression goes, *"le pire des étrangers viennent de Paris"*—the worst foreigners come from Paris.

Part of this aversion to outsiders is nothing more than an extreme degree of the normal narrow-minded response any outsider would encounter in any rural area. I don't suppose that if I moved from midtown New York to a tiny village in rural New England that I'd find a very different welcome from what the stranger receives when confronted with the xenophobia of *La France Profonde*.

But Midi village response to outsiders also stems from history. For almost 150 years, this region was a frequent killing field that shifted from Catholic to Protestant hands and back again, leaving tens of thousands dead with each change. If villagers are suspicious of outsiders it was for good reasons—and bad habits don't change much.

There's also a constant reminder of that most irksome of French habits, unrelenting "logic"—or at least the French brand of what is an otherwise rational train of thought. Rule one of life in France: When a Frenchman tells you *"c'est logique,"* you know you're in deep trouble.

Much of the aforementioned may strike readers as being little more than in the realm of the mundane or quasi-mundane, the picayune problems of tourists and self-proclaimed expatriates, the paltry piddlings of daily life among the French, what might be summed up philosophically as *"les absurdités de la vie"*—the absurdities of life.

Yet without understanding the absurdities of life among the French, without understanding *les petits problèmes* of this one-thousand-year-old nation and the foreigners who confront it, one cannot possibly understand *les grands problèmes* that face and form the French psyche. And without knowledge of that, one certainly cannot understand why in the world they seem to dislike us so very much—and have done so for so very long. That comes in the next chapter.

CHAPTER THREE

✤ ✤ ✤

A Long Legacy of Love and Hate

Let's face it. The French have been ticked off at us for almost three hundred years. Long before Iraq, long before the Kyoto Accord, long before EuroDisney invaded the French countryside, long before we began to poison the world with McDonald's and GMOs (genetically modified organisms). *En verité,* France's sense of political frustration and national anger with America predates the Declaration of Independence!

Consider the strife-torn history of colonial North America. Both the seventeenth and eighteenth centuries witnessed a steady stream of sharp Anglo-French religious, political, and ethnic rivalries regularly punctuated by outright battles and bloodshed between French Catholic and British Protestant settlers—deadly rivalries that did not end even when England finally managed to push the French out of Canada and the rest of continental North

America (unless you count those silly little rocky islands of St. Pierre et Miquelon).

France was still licking its wounds from the Seven-Year War when the Yankee colonies finally got fed up with England's high-handed colonial rule (not to mention its taxation without representation) and revolted against the Red Coats.

It's hard to believe that amid the heavily perfumed delights of Versailles (they had to be perfumed, nobody bathed), King Louis XVI and his coterie of powder-faced dandies expressed much intrinsic interest in, let alone enthusiasm for, a bunch of *Anglais*-speaking roughneck revolutionaries in the savage woodlands across the Atlantic. Besides, in theory, the kingdom of France was neutral.

But any opportunity to possibly slip back into a North American power position and to tweak King George III's bright red nose in the process was too great a temptation for any blue-blooded Frenchman to resist. "The inveterate enmity of [Britain] imposes upon us the duty to lose no occasion of weakening it," the Comte de Vergennes, Louis's foreign minister, informed his monarch. "We must therefore give support to the independence of the insurgent colonies."

Accordingly, the Court of Versailles took its revenge on the Court of St. James's by receiving no one less than Benjamin Franklin in Paris. With great fanfare, the French king told the wise old Philadelphian that he was prepared to conclude an alliance promising that France would fight Britain alongside the Yankees until American independence was guaranteed. Most important, Louis said, he would begin supplying the American rebel forces with the arms, supplies, and military manpower that would prove decisive in our eventual victory.

In 1777, eight chartered ships set sail from France loaded with two hundred brass cannons; three hundred rifles; one hundred tons of powder; three thousand tents; bullets, mortars, and cannonballs; and enough clothing for thirty thousand men. Above all, France sent well-trained French troops, a commodity the Yankees needed almost as desperately as supplies.

The French reinforcements were received with predictable Yankee enthusiasm. "The French officers are the most civilized men I have ever met," reported one enthralled New England merchant. Another advised that their appearance belied British propaganda. "Neither officers nor men are the effeminate Beings we were heretofore taught to believe."

Moreover, while today's rash of anti-French jokes make much of the French military's World War II penchant for rapid retreat and swift surrender, at least during the Revolutionary War, the French more than proved their value as fighters. Consider this: At the all important Battle of Yorktown, eighteen thousand French seamen and seventy-eight hundred French troops fought the British under the French flag—more than three times as many Continental troops and militiamen who fought there under the American flag. And they defeated the Redcoats!

Unfortunately, the spirit of Lafayette and the Comte de Rochambeau, who had come to Washington's aid with a French fleet and six thousand hard-fighting troops, was soon to fade. At the 1783 peace negotiations that Paris hosted between the Americans and British, the American representatives—Benjamin Franklin, John Jay, and John Adams—discovered to their horror that for all their glad-handedness, the shifty French were secretly ignoring some vital American interests and even trying to deny Washington valuable fishing rights off Newfoundland.

Severely miffed, Ben Franklin must have consulted his own copy of *Poor Richard's Almanac* and decided that indeed, "God helps them that help themselves." And to the outrage of the French, the Americans began dealing directly with the British.

Zut alors! Still, the French swallowed their pride and eventually succeeded in brokering a treaty that assured American independance. Their hope: Once they'd accomplished that, the newborn United States would be so grateful that it would become a staunch ally that could help France contain the hated *Anglais* forevermore.

Once again the United States disappointed the French. When the French Revolution broke out in 1786 and Parisian mobs began to loot palaces and lop off aristocratic heads, Washington proved decidedly cool. And when actual war broke out between newly Republican France and Royal England in 1793, America simply refused to join in on its French ally's side.

This time the French were really furious. To smooth out the rancor, President John Adams sent a special mission to Paris in 1797. Things went from bad to worse when the French foreign minister, Charles-Maurice de Talleyrand-Périgord, gauchely demanded a bribe to make things right. Adams undiplomatically blew his powdered wig and exposed the affair, helping to trigger a two-year Franco-American unofficial war at sea that ended only with the formal abrogation of young America's first "entangling" alliance with France.

It did not, however, end France's dream of reestablishing a North American bridgehead. No one less than Napoleon Bonaparte envisioned the first step by regaining control of Louisiana from Spain, something he actually managed to do in November 1803.

But the best-laid plans of mice and emperors often go astray. A bloody slave rebellion in Haiti and Napoleon's fear that New Orleans would fall into British hands in an impending war forced the little emperor to reshuffle his priorities. In December 1803, just a month after he got it back from the Spaniards, Napoleon embarrassingly sold the Louisiana territories to the United States for $15 million.

American ships proved easy targets for both sides in this newest of the long list of Anglo-French wars. But the French seized and sank fewer Yankee clippers than did the British, so in 1812 the United States finally declared war on the British and fought as a sort of ally of the French.

Nonetheless, the French continued to perceive the Americans as nothing less than pushy upstarts and a continued obstacle to French ambitions in the Western Hemisphere. "James Monroe

enunciated his Doctrine in 1823," writes veteran Paris-based journalist Mort Rosenblum in his book *Mission to Civilize: The
French Way,* "prompting L'Etoile in Paris to reflect on the cheeki-
ness of a temporary president of a poorly armed republic, independent for only forty years."

Worse yet, the Monroe Doctrine seemed to align the United
States with Britain in a move to block continental European powers from the Americas.

There were further French exasperations with Washington
throughout the nineteenth century, and as a result, there was a
decided French preference for the Confederacy during the American Civil War. Napoleon III allowed ships to be built in France
for the Confederacy and even helped the cash-strapped rebels
float major loans.

France also used America's preoccupation with its civil strife to
slip back into the New World; the French established a puppet
emperor in Mexico, Maximillian of Austria, and dispatched
French troops to occupy America's southern neighbor. Abraham
Lincoln was not amused, but was otherwise occupied. When the
Civil War ended, the United States sent General Philip Sheridan
and his troops to rattle swords along the Mexican border. The
French got the hint and retreated; Maximillian was executed by
the Mexicans.

Less than two decades later, some French went out of their way
to show cordiality and friendship by presenting America with the
monumental Statue of Liberty, an idea dreamed up by a wealthy

Americanophile named Edouard de Laboulaye who formed a Franco-American Union to raise funds for the giant statue that was forged in Paris and shipped across the Atlantic in 214 crates.

But French historians like Philippe Roger, author of *L'ennemi Américain,* believe that Lady Liberty notwithstanding, real trauma hit France with the 1898 Spanish-American War. As Roger sees it, the French interpreted the American attack on Spain as "the beginning of an American War with Europe—a war that the Old World might lose."

Roger and other French analysts also believed that France not only perceived American political power as a surrogate of the reviled British and a hostile political force, but deeply feared that the strength and dynamics of the growing American economy challenged France's set ways and threatened to overshadow it— as, in fact, it eventually did. America's "absolute capitalism," as the French political world began to sarcastically call it, was seen and is still seen as one of America's greatest abominations—the reflection of an uncaring, unbridled American urge to grow at any cost.

The fact that America was a land of immigrants also played into the hands of France's xenophobic nationalists, especially its increasingly influential political strata of nineteenth-century anti-Semites. These defenders of the faith saw wealthy German-American Jews like Jacob Schiff as particular enemies of La France Chretienne. As the Council on Foreign Relations's Walter Mead wrote in *Foreign Affairs:* "partly because of the belief that Jews ran the American financial system, a generation of Frenchmen grew up thinking of Uncle Sam as *'Oncle Shylock.'"*

Such attitudes echo even in today's France, where elements of both the French Left and Right firmly believe that a cabal of wily Jews controls not only American finance but also American foreign policy, especially with regard to Iraq and the rest of the Middle East.

That congenital French suspicion of Jews, especially American Jews, says *International Herald Tribune* editor Walter Wells, is a central root of French anti-Americanism. "Many Americans have the impression," says Wells, "that anti-Americanism in France is a disguised form of anti-Semitism. The French dislike American foreign policy because it favors Israel; if the Americans did not favor Israel, the world would somehow be less complicated, less troublesome. It is another manner of enunciating an old and sad reality: this marvelous country of human rights [France] sent many thousands of Jews to die in Germany, not without a certain pleasure."

Yet twenty-five years earlier, in World War I, when France faced the invading Germans, America had sailed to its rescue, albeit somewhat belatedly. Though at first America sought ways to remain neutral, pro-French passions soon ran high. Irving Berlin and the other whiz kids of Tin Pan Alley produced a steady flurry of catchy song hits geared to stir support for the battles already raging "Over There." Most had a decidedly pro-French, remember-our-debt-to-dear-Old-France pitch: "Lafayette, We

Hear You Calling . . . America Is Coming," "France We Have Not Forgotten You," and scores of other maudlin melodies.

Pro-German propaganda did exist, but it made little impression on the general public. Most Americans saw the Germans as "Huns," baby-bayoneting foot soldiers of a dangerous monarchy with autocratic militarist thinking, including a hidden agenda to undermine democracy and U.S. power. There were allegations of industrial sabotage, poisoning water supplies, kidnapping individuals, and engaging in espionage within American labor unions by Germans to keep the United States busy on the home front. These rumors, along with extensive submarine warfare against American ships, added to the distrust of the Germans and the growing support for the allies.

America finally declared war on Germany on April 6, 1917. And once again Tin Pan Alley accommodated by stirring our souls with songs like my all-time favorite: "You'll Find Old Dixieland in France":

> *Instead of pickin' melons off the vine,*
> *They're pickin' Germans off the Rhine,*
> *You'll find Old Dixieland in France . . .*

Little matter that the more than two million American doughboys (and girls) who sang "Goodbye Broadway—Hello France" did not see any combat action at the front lines until October of 1917, and that most American-made armaments, and especially air materials, did not reach the front lines until well into 1918, just months before the war ended. In the meantime, France had lost an astounding 1.4 million men, one every second from 1914 to 1918. No village in France was spared the sacrifice of its sons, and the staggering loss would traumatize the French for generations.

Even so, it was the American entry into the war—and the American loss of 116,000 men—that added just enough weight to tip the final balance in favor of the Allies and save France from defeat. (Though not enough for America to be mentioned in France's annual Armistice Day celebrations each November 11.)

Washington and Paris clashed at the Versailles postwar peace conference over debt repayment and ways to keep Germany in check. Ironically enough, postures at Versailles were reversed with the United States trying to play the role the French currently claim to have assumed for themselves: the champion of a moral, legal peace.

The story is told of a candlelit dinner in the magnificent Hall of Mirrors. President Woodrow Wilson was pontificating about the ethical power of "justice through international law." Finally, Georges Clemenceau, the old walrus-mustached premier of France, is said to have turned to Wilson and asked, "M. le Président, do you see that chicken on your plate?"

Wilson glanced down at his elegant portion of pressed coq and rare mushrooms and nodded.

"Alors," said Clemenceau, "international law never helped him."

Despite the difference, and our inability to join France in the League of Nations, the interwar years saw a blooming of Franco-

American friendship. France was the in place, and during the Roaring Twenties and early thirties, the cream of America's intellectuals and artists flocked to Paris and the Riviera to taste deeply of its wine, food, art, and free-spirited living. They were the years of Ernest Hemingway's "moveable feast."

"We felt as though we were in the center of a new and exciting universe," recalled Mary Jane Gold, a Chicago heiress and aviatrix who came to Paris as a party girl and eventually worked in an early American rescue network that helped refugees like Marc Chagall flee from the Nazis.

The French for their part discovered American talents, especially those in their midst: from Gertrude Stein to William Faulkner to Josephine Baker to Tom Mix to Frank Lloyd Wright—all had profound effects upon the face of modern French culture.

France itself was in political turmoil—at one point during the Third Republic, the French had seventeen different governments over seven years. And the United States was struggling with a decimating depression.

The long shadow of the Nazi threat brought the two nations closer still, and when Hitler invaded France in 1940 it was clear where America's sympathies lay. But the embarrassing speed with which the French defense crumbled shocked most Americans—as did the seeming preference of a majority of Frenchmen to collaborate openly or placidly rather than resist.

Faced with that harsh reality, Franklin D. Roosevelt at first recognized the French facist regime led by Marshal Philippe Pétain—

hoping it would sway the Vichy government to swing to the Allied cause. When that failed, and after the United States had entered the war, Roosevelt ordered his air force to join the British in attacking the Vichy sea and land bases in North Africa—an event some Frenchmen still criticize. That and other aspects of anti-Americanism echo despite the fact that the United States saved France from defeat three times during the twentieth century: World War I, World War II, and the postwar years when communism was a serious threat to the survival of French republicanism.

At the urging of Winston Churchill, Roosevelt eventually opened the White House door to the forces of Free France, led by a young general named Charles de Gaulle. De Gaulle saw himself as no ordinary mortal. He was Eternal France incarnate, a latter-day Charlemagne who would lead his nation to new triumphs.

To many Americans, though, de Gaulle seemed nothing more than a haughty anachronism, a stiff-necked narcissist who was determined to spite the United States at every turn. He was a classic of French arrogance, an egotist—serving himself while serving France. And much if not most of his postwar attitude toward the United States was formed during World War II and was rooted in his sour relationship with Franklin D. Roosevelt, who at first accepted de Gaulle as the only game in town but then grew to neither like the tall lank French general nor trust him.

As far as FDR was concerned, de Gaulle was far too independent for a man whose nation had so easily knuckled under to the Germans. "One of the meanest SOBs to ever straddle a pot" was how one of FDR's closest aides remembered him being described. And FDR resented both the Frenchman's airs as well as his attempt to cooperate with the Allies only when it suited him and his postwar ambitions. "My grandfather thought that de Gaulle had the potential and the hubris to try to become another Napoleon," recalls FDR's eldest grandson, Curtis Roosevelt, who now lives in the south of France. "FDR thought de Gaulle might unilaterally and without democratic process establish himself as the head of government of postwar France."

FDR especially blamed de Gaulle for the almost total lack of organized French resistance to the Germans or Vichy in North Africa, something Roosevelt believed had unnecessarily cost American and British lives.

De Gaulle, for his part, always resented Roosevelt's initial attempts to sway the Vichy government to the anti-Nazi side. And de Gaulle was well aware of Roosevelt's personal disdain for him. He also knew well that members of the Roosevelt administration were eager to see him sidestepped. Secretary of State Sumner Welles once even suggested that the only way to save the Free France movement was by "divesting" de Gaulle of his power. In fact, Roosevelt so doubted the loyalty of de Gaulle that he and Churchill kept the Anglo-American invasion of North Africa a secret from him, not to mention the Normandy landings, and cut him out of the Yalta Conference.

"This incompatibility," wrote Milton Viorst in his 1965 book *Hostile Allies,* "which revealed so much of these men and the countries they led, contains the roots of the American difference with France today."

De Gaulle wasted no time in showing us which way the French wind was blowing. Maybe we were just too busy celebrating. But we should have known just what we were going to be up against from the very day Paris was liberated on August 25, 1944.

Fearing that battles between retreating German troops and euphoric young French street fighters would leave the City of Lights in ruins, General Charles de Gaulle had urgently entreated Allied Supreme Commander Dwight David Eisenhower to send troops to liberate Paris as soon as possible. Ike agreed and as a diplomatic gesture to the French, the Free French Second Armored Division was dispatched together with backup units of the tough U.S. Fourth Division. A clear line of march was laid out for both to follow.

But the haughty, unsmiling de Gaulle had his own scheme. To the annoyance of Ike and his staff, de Gaulle and his deputy, General Jean Jacques-Phillipe Leclerc, ignored the Allied march plan. The French troops swung eastward and entered Paris through the southern Port d'Orleans without any American GIs to share the triumph of being the first to enter the liberated French capital.

Within hours de Gaulle was standing on the balcony of the Hôtel de Ville, the wedding cake–like Paris City Hall. "Paris liberated!" he regally proclaimed to the cheering crowds below. "Liberated by herself, liberated by her people, in concurrence with the armies of France, with the support and concurrence of the whole of France, of fighting France, the only France, the true France, eternal France."

Nary a mention of Americans, Canadians, British, Dutch, Australians, or any other Allied troops who'd landed only weeks before on the beaches of Normandy and were, even as the general spoke, still slogging their way through occupied France.

The public response to the American liberation of France is still viewable in those grainy black-and-white newsreel shots of GIs being ecstatically welcomed with flowers, bottles of wine, and the wet kisses of dozens of delirious mademoiselles. But it didn't last. "While nobody denied the role played by American forces in the Allied victory, reactions to a continuing American presence in France at the Liberation were not favorable," says Professor John Flower of the University of Kent in England. "Opinion polls show that the majority of French people felt that America's attitude towards Germany was likely to be too conciliatory and there were many who could neither forget nor forgive the Americans' bombing of towns like Royan and Le Havre."

Flower points out that French opposition came especially from the Left. America was accused by the French Communist Party of imperialism and of being a threat to world peace. "Countless articles and cartoons in the Communist paper *Les Lettres francaises,* for example, portrayed the American presence as a repetition of the Nazi occupation. A few intellectuals such as Raymond Aron viewed America with approval, but on the whole they were wary.

America and American culture were seen as shallow, typified by Coca-Cola, jeans and the *Reader's Digest.*"

There was even a Communist move to have Coca-Cola outlawed.

Meanwhile, at the urging of de Gaulle, France struggled to close its ranks even if it meant forgiving most of its *collabos,* traitors. Pierre Laval was shot, and Pétain sent to prison. But Maurice Papon, a senior civil servant in the Vichy regime who was directly responsible for the deportation to Auschwitz of fifteen hundred Jews, including two hundred children, became chief of the Paris police under de Gaulle, and a cabinet minister under Valery Giscard d'Estaing. The young François Mitterrand, who had once served the Vichy government himself, renewed his personal ties to René Bousquet, the Vichy's chief of police, ties that Mitterrand refused to sever even when he became president of the republic.

Cooperation and discord marked the postwar years. The U.S. Marshall Plan helped breathe life back into the ailing French economy, and in the process helped prevent France from becoming yet another Soviet satellite. When the North Atlantic Treaty was signed in 1949, France and the United States again became formal allies. But the American government strongly disapproved of France's colonial wars in North Africa and Southeast Asia. So much so that, in 1954, Dwight D. Eisenhower refused to help save French troops at the siege of Dien Bien Phu.

Both countries were united in Cold War confrontations with the Soviet Union, albeit with ambiguous nuances of their own.

But after Charles de Gaulle became president in 1958, he squabbled with Washington over such issues as his decision to build a solo French nuclear arsenal and Britain's admission to the European Common Market. The major crisis came over France's role in the North Atlantic Treaty Organization (NATO). De Gaulle announced that he was unilaterally withdrawing France from active military participation in NATO and wanted U.S. troops out of France—a move that prompted Secretary of State Dean Rusk to ask de Gaulle, "Should we dig up our dead in Normandy and take them home, too?"

The French Right disapproved of America's war in Vietnam, an area they still considered their own sphere of influence; the Left vehemently opposed it. And as the French Left and Right struggled to hold or seize power from one another, America became an increasingly comfortable scapegoat for both sides. Yet, like it or not, there was no realpolitik way to avoid American global leadership. Like it or not, the Soviet threat was real and America the major protector against it. The French were reduced to flitting around America like an annoying mosquito in the night.

"As long as there was a visible security threat and nowhere else for the Europeans to go," says centrist French parliamentarian Pierre Lellouche, "they simply had to accept U.S. leadership even if they disagreed with it. There were crises and France was always at the forefront of those crises. There were confrontations on trade and economic issues, on nuclear strategy and so on. No question about it. But they couldn't break the U.S. guarantees.

Nobody in Europe saw France as a credible alternative to America. All the French attempts to federate Europe as a counterweight to the U.S. never worked.

"The end of the Cold War changed all that," says Lellouche, a leader of France's UMP (Union Pour un Mouvement Populaire) party. "Suddenly the fundamental cement was gone. And if today we are in a different war, a war against terrorism, the Europeans and especially the French don't want to realize that."

CHAPTER FOUR

✤ ✤ ✤

Hinky, Dinky *Parlez-Vous:*
France's War on Terror

France's participation in the global war on terror has been about as enthusiastic and effective as its 1940 defense along the Maginot Line.

While the rest of the civilized world has launched an increasingly united front against international terrorism, the French have stuck stubbornly to their old *moi*-first game, all too often selfishly covering their own *derrières* while ignoring terrorist threats to longtime friends and allies.

Amazingly—or perhaps not so amazingly—they have developed a tradition of trying to strike their own separate deals with terrorist organizations. On more than one occasion, French security services have even turned a blind eye to the presence in France itself of leading international terrorists. As investigative author Kenneth Timmerman says, "France has repeatedly negotiated with terrorists, their representatives, their proxies, and their supporters, in the vain hope of preventing further terrorist attacks on French soil or against French citizens abroad."

Some intelligence agencies are convinced, for example, that in the late 1960s, the French negotiated an unpublished arrangement with the Palestine Liberation Organization (PLO): "We'll let you operate quietly in France if you promise not to carry on operations here."

That may explain why Mohammed Daoud Odeh, the notorious chief of the PLO hit squad that slaughtered eleven Israeli athletes at the 1972 Munich Olympics, was invited by the French government to come to Paris to meet with senior Quai d'Orsay officials in early 1977.

When word leaked out that this stellar terrorist (a.k.a. Abu Daoud) was in town, American, German, and Israeli intelligence agencies frantically sought French help in nabbing him. But before any joint action could be taken to grab this murderer, the government of then president Valery Giscard d'Estaing swept down on Abu Daoud's safe house, "arrested" him, and, before you could say "Yasir Arafat," hustled him off to a Paris airport where he was safely placed aboard a flight that took him to the shelter of terrorist-loving Algeria.

The Socialist presidency of François Mitterrand and the conservative presidency of Jacques Chirac that followed have both found occasion to dance the terrorist tango. Both administrations stuck to the self-centered, cynical politics of their predecessors. During the 1980s, one of the world's most wanted terrorist criminals made so many trips to Paris that he probably could have earned enough frequent-flier miles for a visit to New York.

Lebanese Hezbollah leader Imad Mugniyah is the man who tortured and murdered U.S. Navy diver Robert Stethem aboard the hijacked TWA flight 847 in June of 1985, and is believed to have kidnapped, tortured, and later murdered William Buckley, the CIA station chief in Beirut in 1984–85.

According to several sources, including investigative reporter Timmerman, a Central Intelligence Agency operative photographed Mugniyah—who was also one of the men held responsible for the death of sixty-three people in the bombing of the U.S. embassy in Beirut on April 18, 1983—arriving at Orly Airport in Paris in 1985. "They passed the photographs to the French in an unsuccessful effort to get them to arrest him."

Non-French Western intelligence agencies, especially the CIA, were outraged. "The French refusal to grab Mugniyah was as disgusting as it was criminal," one Western intelligence source tells me. For not only had Mugniyah attacked American and Israeli targets, he was also blamed for planning the October 23, 1983, simultaneous truck bombings against U.S. Marine and French paratrooper barracks in Beirut, a Hezbollah action that killed 58 French soldiers and 241 U.S. marines, sailors, and soldiers.

Armed by Iran, supported by Syria, and based in Lebanon, Hezbollah has a well-earned reputation as one of the most blood-drenched of the anti-Western Muslim terrorist organizations. Until the tragedy of September 11, 2001, Hezbollah held the dubious distinction of having kidnapped and killed more Americans than any other terrorist organization. Richard Armitage, the outspoken U.S. deputy secretary of state, was once quoted as saying that Hezbollah is "the A-team of terrorists, while Al Qaeda may actually be the B-team."

But that murderous reputation and even the memory of the French servicemen Hezbollah buried under tons of rubble in the Beirut bombings failed to prevent France from lobbying ferociously in the European Union bloc against adding Hezbollah to the European Union's list of international terrorist organizations. Nor did it seem to weigh at all on Jacques Chirac's conscience when the French president personally extended an invitation to Sheikh Hassan Nasrallah, Hezbollah's secretary general, to attend a French-sponsored summit of Francophone (French-speaking) nations in Beirut in October 2002.*

The cruel irony is that for all its shameful record of appeasement of terrorists, for all its diplomatic efforts to suck up to Arab states, France has been unable to fully protect itself or its citizens from terrorism. Like a growing number of nations, France and French interests have been subject to terrorist hijackings—most notorious, that of the Air France plane to Uganda in 1976 (which Israeli commandos freed at Entebbe), and another in 1994 that the would-be hijackers were purported to be planning to crash into the Eiffel Tower. Yet another plane was blown up over the

---

*France did finally ban Hezbollah's racist television channel from using French satellites.

Sahara in 1989, killing all passengers, most of them French citizens.

French journalists have also not been immune to kidnappings by Arab terrorists—both in Lebanon and more recently in Iraq where, despite Chirac's appeasement policy, Islamic radicals nabbed two French correspondents and threatened to execute them if France did not rescind its restrictions on girls wearing Islamic scarves in public schools—a ruling that is in line with France's strict separation of church and state. Their capture was not without its own irony: Both journalists, especially *Figaro*'s George Malbrunet, were known for their frequent overtly pro-Arab reporting.

The dismayed French government responded by sending delegations of French Muslims to Baghdad to plead for their release—and by constantly conjuring up France's "friendship" with the Arab world. The two were finally released after four months, but it is unclear whether or how much ransom was paid for them.

Nor has the French homeland itself been spared. Throughout the eighties and into the nineties, Paris itself rocked to a series of bloody bombings in streets, restaurants, cafés, and the underground Métro—all of them the work of Islamic extremists.

Attacks have also occurred against diplomatic representatives in France of the United Arab Emirates and Saudi Arabia. France's ever cozy relations with the secular regimes of the Middle East have even encouraged terrorism, as supporters of these governments have often been targeted by religious extremists. And according to French intelligence sources, France, a nation with a 10 percent population of Muslims, now faces a real nightmare: a growing sleeper network of Islamic extremists, including clerics who use local French mosques to extol the virtues of "sacrifice."

So is this French masochism? Some kind of twisted Gallic desire to wallow in self-destruction?

No, it is just another searing example of French arrogance on the international stage, another famous French moment in self-deceptive diplomacy. For in their manic myopia, the French remain convinced that they are the exception, they can be immune from terror. Why? Because once upon a long time ago they had a rich history of ties, influence, and colonial control in North Africa and the Middle East. As a result, goes French thinking, it is they, more than anyone else, who know how best to deal with the nations, governments, and even terrorists of the Middle East.

"The problem," a French diplomat once earnestly told me, "is that you Americans really don't know how to handle the Arabs; you lack sensitivity to their culture, to their values and to their perspective on life and world politics. We, on the other hand, know them and understand them. We have a natural affinity, a *savoir faire,* if you will."

Zut alors! It must be that same affinity and deep understanding, that same *savoir faire* that resulted in France being forced to place its tail securely between its legs and flee its former colonies in Morocco, Algeria, and Tunisia—a move that also resulted in the displacement of one million *pied-noirs,* French residents of

North Africa who were forced to flee to the homeland leaving their properties and belongings behind.

Similar Mideast acumen led to France's loss of its power holds in both Syria and Lebanon—not to mention its once healthy influence over Egypt.

And *sans doute,* it is this same deep sensitivity to international justice that has driven France to become the loudest member of Europe's anti-Israel cheering squad, a position expressed ad nauseum by the French political world and by the French media, a criticism that is ofttimes so virulent that one gets the impression that if only Israel—arguably America's firmest friend in the Middle East—would agree to eliminate itself from the Mideast map, Osama bin Laden himself would offer to join the French Foreign Legion and we would immediately be able to cure the world of Islamic terrorism in all its forms.

Knee-jerk French criticism of Israel wasn't always the order of the day. During the early years of Israel's existence and struggle to survive, France was actually among its most fervent supporters. Some argue that at least part of that policy was motivated by a subliminal sense of remorse for France's own role in the Holocaust. I believe it was more likely a pragmatic means to an end: a way to counter British and growing American influence in the Middle East, and to regain control of the Suez Canal, lost when Egypt's Gamal Abdel Nasser nationalized it.

Whatever the case, French aircraft and arms sales to the Jewish state, for example, did much to help it win the Six-Day War of

1967; France also supplied Israel with some of its earliest nuclear know-how.

During a visit to Paris in those heady days, Israel's tough and usually realistic founding father David Ben-Gurion once naively told Charles de Gaulle that Israel considered France its "best friend and most sincere ally." The ever aloof de Gaulle couldn't resist cutting Ben-Gurion down. "France," he reportedly proclaimed to the somewhat crestfallen Israeli leader, "has no friends, enemies or allies; it only has interests."

Predictably, then, the moment de Gaulle felt it would best serve French interests, he changed that pro-Israel policy with one fell swoop. The haughty general believed France could reestablish its long-lost power position by countering both the Americans and the Soviets and forming a bloc of Third World and neutral nations that *naturellement* France would lead. His first candidates for this neo-Gaullist empire of influence were countries in France's traditional spheres of influence: Africa and the Middle East, especially with Arab states who were then within or on the edge of the Soviet web of influence.

Arab leaders seemed quite interested at first in this Gaullist shuffle of world politics. Though most warmly welcomed Soviet arms and paid the political price by supporting the Soviet Union on the international stage, none of them wanted to be dominated by either superpower, and all looked positively on France's policy of trying to balance the United States and the U.S.S.R. France's former colonies in eastern and northern Africa already maintained close economic and cultural ties to France, and were rarely courted by the major powers. They were delighted with the attention France showered on them, not to mention the goodies that came to them as part of the package.

There was one major problem: France was still involved in a savage war against Algerian rebels. That didn't sit too well with the Arab states that France was trying to court. But when de Gaulle finally surrendered to Algeria's Muslim FLN separatists in 1962, and granted France's former Sahara colony independence, it seemed the last real barrier between France and its new friendship with the Arab world disappeared.

All, that is, but one: French support for Israel.

Faced with that challenge to French honor and decency, de Gaulle overturned France's Mideast policy and turned his back on Israel, then the West's most effective Mideast bulwark against Soviet power. He chose the spring of 1967—just as Egypt, Syria, Jordan, and the rest of the Arab world were threatening the Jewish state with a "war of annihilation"—to make the change known.

Despite personal pleas from Ben-Gurion that Israel's very existence was at stake, de Gaulle and his government publicly opposed any Israeli preemptive action, announced he was cutting off French support for Israel, and imposed an embargo on arms supplies. When the Jewish state did launch a preemptive strike rather than wait for the Arabs to overrun it as the Germans had overrun France in 1940, de Gaulle was livid and angrily castigated Israel for ignoring his advice.

Israel's terrible swift sword defeated the Arab armies in those historic six days of that monumental Mideast war. Though French public opinion then was largely in Israel's favor, official France wasted no time in bitterly condemning Israel's occupation of the West Bank and Gaza. Paris refused to recognize Israel's reunification of Jerusalem and in an outrageous quote that still haunts his memory, de Gaulle pointedly and publicly denounced the Jews and Israel as "an elite people, sure of itself and domineering."

In other words, those pushy Jews had ignored de Gaulle and the will of France.

The French government continued to criticize Israel and other Israeli actions, including its defensive operations against the terrorist Palestine Liberation Organization. About the same time, France began to use its veto power to oppose Israel in the United Nations. France was now systematically siding with the Arab states on almost all issues brought before the international body.

Most important of all, however, de Gaulle's government refused to revoke the arms embargo on the Jewish state. Theoretically, the embargo was applied to all Mideast combatants. But it wasn't long before the French found a way to begin selling weaponry to the Arab states again. As early as 1970, France sold Libya a hundred Mirage fighter jets. After 1967, France continued to support Israel's right to exist, but it was lip service support and extended little beyond that.

De Gaulle's memoirs show that despite the French bourgeoisie's long history of latent (and sometimes very open) anti-Semitism, the aging general did have some personal sympathy for the Jewish state. But he saw it in the selfish interests of France to distance the two nations. In order to pursue political and economic ends, de Gaulle crafted a pragmatic new Middle Eastern policy that continued minimal support for Israel but traded it in for close relations with the Arabs.

His immense shift in policy was also provoked by his sense that the strengthening alliance between the United States and Israel would, in any case, have eventually made France's role as an ally of Israel mostly irrelevant. The United States could always provide Israel with more money and with higher levels of military technology than France could. Supporting the Arab side would give France more leverage in the region's future.

And there was a lot of money to be made. The French constantly and passionately claim that "principles" rather than that ugly word *profit* are the primary motivations for their state policies. Monetary considerations, they will tell you, are strictly an American aberration.

Right!

In fact, France and its economic czars saw in the Arab world an enormous potential for a hyper-healthy boost to French trade as well as French political influence. "Just look at the demographic statistics," one French official eagerly told me in 1969. In the late sixties, the Arab states had a combined population of over one hundred million; tiny Israel had only three million.

But ironically, aside from arms and oil deals, France initially had little trade success in the Arab world. Despite the fact that none of them were as outspokenly pro-Arab as France, the United States, Britain, and West Germany still sold far more to the Middle East than did France. *Au contraire.* Both America and Britain strongly supported anti-Soviet Israel and were no friends of several important Soviet-friendly Arab governments—notably that of Egypt's Gamal Abdel Nasser. Problem was, nothing from France could compete with Anglo-American prices.

That changed only after France had reached new levels of economic success. Accordingly, the French government allowed itself to make major increases in foreign-aid spending. So much so, in fact, that France become second only to the United States in total aid among the Western powers. By the end of the sixties, France was paying out close to a billion dollars a year in aid—far more than either West Germany or the United Kingdom. Though the total amount still paled in comparison to U.S. spending, France paid the most per capita in foreign aid of any of the major powers. And the vast majority of this French benevolence was directed toward Africa and the Middle East. France also increased its expenditures on other forms of aid, sending out skilled individuals to developing countries to provide technical expertise—and make heroic efforts to leave the French cultural and political imprints on local lands.

The combination of aid money, arms sales, and new alignments and diplomatic coziness helped France to erase the Arab world's angry memory of the Suez Crisis and the Algerian War. Indeed, France successfully developed warm ties with the governments of many of the Middle Eastern states. Egyptian dictator Gamal Abdel Nasser and de Gaulle, who shared many similarities in style of rule, cooperated together in attempts to limit American power in the region. Nasser proclaimed France "the only friend" Egypt had in the West. France's relations with its former colony Syria were improved, and eroded cultural links were partially restored.

Most important, France and Iraq also developed a close relationship with the increasingly dangerous regime of Iraq and Saddam Hussein. These included business ties, joint military training exercises, arms supplies, and eventually French assistance in Iraq's nuclear program in the 1970s.

With the deals piling up and the coffers filling up, strategists at the Élysée Palace and the Quai d'Orsay decided that there was even more money as well as political hay to be made in the Arab world by becoming even more anti-Israeli. A decision appears to have been taken to shift strategy again and intensify French criticism of the Jewish state.

With increasing velocity to this day, the French stance has morphed from one that was supposedly "even-handed" to one that is undeniably overtly pro-Arab and stridently, even enthusiastically, captious of Israel. So much so, in fact, that while anti-Zionism has become popular and commonplace on both the European Left and Right, in France it has become political orthodoxy with dangerous overtones that as political commentator Alexandre Adler puts it, "seem to license anti-Semitism."

Israel bashing has also become a convenient French mechanism for yet further jabs at France's most favorite target: the United States. As the French argument goes, failure to achieve a peace settlement in the Middle East is due mainly to American support for Israeli "intransigence." It is an argument that has an especially wide echo among the French intellectual classes who have concluded that Israel, as well as America, represent the world's biggest threats to peace.

French diplomatic attacks on Israel now reach new high levels of tendentiousness both in public forums and even behind closed doors of otherwise genteel social gatherings. In 2003, France's ambassador to England was quoted as referring to Israel at a swank London dinner party as that "shitty little country"—a comment he never denied. "Why should we be in danger of World War III because of *those people*?" the undiplomatic diplomat asked rhetorically. The French ambassador never apologized nor was he recalled or even publicly chastised by the Quai d'Orsay.

More recently, former French foreign minister Michel Rocard went out of his way to suggest at an international conference held at the Alexandria Biblioteque, Egypt's impressive new national library, that the very decision to establish a Jewish homeland may well have been a mistake. There was nary a word of criticism in the French press.

Le Monde published a cartoon captioned "History Repeats,"

equating an Israeli assault on part of a West Bank town in which Palestinian suicide bombers were based with the Nazi incineration of the Warsaw Ghetto in which three hundred thousand noncombatant Jews were annihilated.

The net result of this campaign has not been to enhance French prestige but to dishonor it. A recent cogent editorial by the *Jerusalem Post's* Sarah Honig spelled it out clearly: "If appearing to take umbrage, sucking up to its burgeoning Muslim electorate, currying favor with genocidally minded Arab oil potentates, or demonizing Israel serves France's immediate purposes, then all the above not only become its policy but are pretentiously presented as higher principles. In their name, French officialdom fulminates with vehement indignation whenever it's determined that Israel again gave offense. Yet reactions to terror are temperate and remote. This cannot but feed latent anti-Semitism."

Indeed, while I believe that not all criticism of Israeli government policy equates with anti-Semitism, the vehemence of French policy has given license to hate. Since the end of the war and the revelations of the Holocaust that killed six million European Jews, it has been politically incorrect in France and elsewhere in Europe to directly attack Jews.

In its steady stream of tendentious attacks on most anything Israel does, in its abiding support for Yasir Arafat and his corrupt coven of thugs, the French have enabled those who might think otherwise to employ unremitting anger at Israel as a metaphor to justify their hatred of Jews. It is this succor that has undoubtedly helped spark the rash of anti-Semitic violence that pervades France today.

In the United States and in the European Parliament, French delegates lead the critique of Israel. Just last year, France went into a near frenzy in an attempt to mobilize European Union delegates at the UN to vote "yes" on the General Assembly resolution calling on Israel to take down the security barrier it was building against Palestinian terror. As the *New Republic*'s Martin Peretz put it, "The French came up with long lists of fatuous reasons to support this demand . . . but the real reason that France and some others oppose the fence is that it works."

France also hung on to the PLO and its corrupt dictator leader Yasir Arafat with all the tenacity of a Parisian poodle in heat. Speaking at a NATO summit in Istanbul, Jacques Chirac solemnly declared that the discredited and now deceased Palestinian dictator was the only legitimate representative of the Palestinian people, and that no Mideast agreement could be signed without him. Small wonder the French fawned over the ailing Arafat, who finally died in a French military hospital and was then given a ceremonial send-off befitting a potentate.

Adds Peretz: "All of France's interventions in the [Mideast] have brought nothing good: more of terror, more of Arafat, worst of all, more of Palestinian suffering, all to succor the illusion of French influence in the region."

Over the past three decades, the French seem to have developed a special soft spot for Arab despots. Among them, Libya's terrorism-loving Muammar Gadhafi. French affection for the crackpot dictator, who wore a gaudy leisure suit designed by Yves St. Laurent when I interviewed him in 1986, wasn't because of his taste in couture. France's aerospace industry has always provided the French with major export income. During the 1980s and 1990s alone, military contracts reportedly comprised more than 60 percent of all French aerospace exports. Libya, with its ocean of oil wealth and ravenous appetite for military hardware, seemed to represent a potential bonanza. Gadhafi had the keys to the coffers.

At first, international sanctions against Libya curtailed French military sales. But they didn't stop a French company from negotiating a lucrative contract to build massive agricultural complexes for the Libyan government. Intelligence sources say the "agricultural complexes" actually turned out to be terrorist training camps. But apparently, when the French realized this, no action was taken to back away from the contracts. To the contrary, there were those within the French government who argued vehemently that despite Gadhafi's clear support for terrorism, there was no point in burning the golden bridge to Libya; after all, they said, the colonel might some day be lured into the French sphere of influence!

Gadhafi himself sharpened enthusiasm for this position by showing he had an inclination to one of the most popular of French political traditions: graft. Shortly after the 1981 election of Socialist president François Mitterrand, the Libyan dictator began authorizing healthy kickbacks to the campaign coffers of the French Socialist Party as well as to the private accounts of some of the president's closest advisers.

And then there was the tale of the Libyan mole. Members of the French counterintelligence agency, the DST, maintain that at great expense, Gadhafi actually installed his own personal representative right inside the Élysée Palace itself. The mole, a French bureaucrat who worked closely at Mitterrand's side, remained in place until eventually others in the president's entourage blew his cover. Colonel Gadhafi's French mole was finally fired in September 1986.

The man and his influence may help explain one of the most ignoble chapters of aberrant French behavior toward America and toward the war on terror: the adamant refusal by Mitterrand and his government to allow U.S. military jets to overfly France during the U.S. punitive raids on Libya in April 1986. The raid came five months *before* Libya's mole was tossed out of the Élysée.

Washington's decision to bomb Libya had not been lightly taken. The Reagan administration was certain that in addition to an increasing propensity to act as the Soviet Union's strawman in Africa, Gadhafi had raised the danger level with his increasing support of international terrorism.

I remember visiting Tripoli in 1986 for my first interview with the crazy colonel. The lobby of the hotel where I stayed was jammed each evening with representatives of terrorist organizations from every corner of the world: Irish separatists, Kurdish nationalists, Palestinian revolutionaries, Sri Lankese bombers—

all were in town waiting for handouts from the Libyans. It was like a terrorist version of the bar scene in *Star Wars.*

Knowing what was at play in Libya, President Ronald Reagan decided to launch a limited air assault. Its goal: to destroy several terrorist training camps and to knock out as many of Libya's military batteries as possible.

Reagan was eager to have France and other Allies participate in the action. At first, François Mitterrand was noncommittal, but then eventually the wily French leader made it clear that while France may not oppose a U.S. strike on Libya, it would not participate in it. "We must avoid everything that could make Gadhafi appear as a hero in the eyes of the Arab world," Mitterrand told Secretary of State George Shultz.

Reagan was furious. Here was the Allied nation whose chestnuts—and just about everything else—we'd pulled out of the fire twice—in 1918 and again in 1944. Why were they not at our side? Ultimately, to save embarrassment, the United States minimized its request: help fulfill the success of the mission by allowing U.S. aircraft to overfly France while en route to Libya.

A steady stream of U.S. officials and unofficials—from Shultz to former secretary of state Henry Kissinger—flew into Paris to plead the American case. But even irrefutable proof that Libya had directed the terrorist bombing of a West Berlin discotheque that had killed one American and injured two hundred others would not sway the French. Both Socialist Mitterrand and his new Conservative prime minister Jacques Chirac, who'd taken office under a power-sharing system the French call *cohabitation,* stood firm. When push came to shove, the shameful but final answer to France's American ally was a resounding *"Non."*

Just as it wouldn't in Iraq, the French refusal to cooperate didn't stop the United States. Late on April 15 and early on April 16, 1986, the United States launched a series of devastating military air strikes against ground targets inside Libya. They were code-named El Dorado Canyon. And even while some of the American planes were still in the sky, President Reagan took to the airwaves to address the world. He emphasized that the action he'd ordered was a matter of U.S. self-defense against Libya's state-sponsored terrorism. "Self-defense is not only our right, it is our duty. It is the purpose behind the mission . . . a mission fully consistent with Article 51 of the UN Charter."

The raid was designed to hit directly at the heart of Gadhafi's ability to export terrorism. It was also hoped that America's preemptive strike would provide the Libyan leader with "incentives and reasons to alter his criminal behavior."

The U.S. choice of targets may have been one of the major factors in dissuading the French from participating or even allowing U.S. overflights. According to Timmerman, who cites a French intelligence source, some of the terrorist training camps the United States planned to destroy had been the very installations a French company had built in the guise of "agricultural complexes." The same French company, claims Timmerman, "was later exposed as a conduit for covert contributions to Mitterrand's Socialist Party. . . . Explaining to Gadhafi how France built the training camps and then joined a U.S. effort to destroy them could get embarrassing."

What did France's cowardice over the Libya raid cost us?

Ultimately, believe experts, the French refusal for twenty-four American FB-11 fighter-bombers to fly over France en route to Libya limited the mission's efficiency. A roundabout route from England, around Gibraltar, and over the Mediterranean had added hours to the run and meant the planes had to be refueled five times. It also increased the risk to the lives of the pilots and ultimately led to some strategic mistakes.

One target "inadvertently" hit during the U.S. raid: the French embassy in Tripoli.

Libya's payback to France came in 1989 when a French airliner with 170 people aboard blew up over the Sahara. The bombing followed a period of tension between Libya and France over borders with Chad, the African nation to the south of Libya that France considers part of its "Francophonic" domain. The bombing occurred at a time when Libya and neighboring Chad were involved in a protracted border dispute. France had made the mistake of supporting Chad in the dispute.

As with the Lockerbie disaster, the Libyans steadfastly denied responsibility, but in 2003, Libya agreed to pay relatives of the French victims $170 million in compensation.

If France's 1986 behavior with Libya was shameful, then its

three-decades-long relationship with Iraq and Saddam Hussein is an as yet unpunished and fully revealed international scandal.

It is now almost thirty years since Jacques Chirac, then the youngest prime minister France ever had, strode out onto the tarmac at Orly Airport to greet a visitor from Baghdad whom he immediately hailed as "my personal friend." It was the thirty-eight-year-old Saddam Hussein, clad in a garish suit and then still nominally Iraq's vice president—though already clearly the most powerful and ruthless man in Baathist Iraq.

In the five red-carpet days that followed, the ambitious Chirac obsequiously wined and dined his visitor, had special *provençal* bullfights laid on for him (Saddam reportedly gave each of the three winners a purse of $200,000), and even invited the Iraqi dictator to his country home.

By the time Saddam boarded his plane for the return to Baghdad, the two *grands amis* had concluded an arms deal that, in fact, they had been negotiating through intermediaries for almost a year. It would mean a guaranteed supply of Iraqi oil for France and monumental investment opportunities for French industry. Most important, it would mean that France could ring up the sale of vast amounts of French arms to Iraq. Included in the deal: the transfer of French treasures of nuclear technology to the ruthless tyrant who would eventually earn the sobriquet The Most Dangerous Man in the World.

It didn't take long for the brutal Iraqi dictator to publicly hail the deal as the first concrete step toward an Arab atomic bomb—a prediction fortunately blown to smithereens in 1981 when the Israeli air force did us all a favor by knocking out the Osiriak installation, the most dangerous of the two French-supplied reactors.

Over the next fifteen years Saddam Hussein would spend upward of $20 billion on French arms and aircraft—and his pal in the Élysée Palace, Jacques Chirac, would justifiably earn the nickname "Ch-iraq."

When Saddam invaded Kuwait in 1990, France chose to temporarily freeze its palsy deals with Iraq and joined the American-led rainbow coalition of Desert Storm that eventually evicted Saddam from the tiny Arab emirate.

Within weeks of the Liberation of Kuwait and the signing of the cease-fire in a desert tent on March 3, 1991, the French were back in Baghdad trying to curry new favor. Saddam, who still referred to Kuwait as Iraq's Nineteenth Province, was desperately trying to rebuild his weapons plants and find spare parts to reequip what was left of his air force. Within months of the end of Desert Storm, Saddam's French-built Mirage fighters were miraculously flying missions along the border of the "no fly" zone. Smuggled goods—some supplied by French middlemen—were flowing into Iraq from the Jordanian port of Aqaba. A French-operated freighter was intercepted carrying chemicals that could be used by Iraq for uranium enrichment. The French, at Saddam's behest, lobbied against the United Nations sea blockade and more and more French businessmen joined the parade of foreign hucksters who once again crowded Baghdad's hotels, smacking their lips in anticipation of new sales to Saddam.

To that end, French diplomats spearheaded the attempt to end the UN's post-Kuwait sanctions system on Saddam's regime. It was certainly a major topic of discussion when the French violated the embargo on Iraq and invited senior Iraqi officials to Paris in 1993 and 1994 to confer with their Quai d'Orsay buddies. Not to be outdone, several major French political figures—from the deputy chairman of the neo-facist National Front Party to Gaullist leader Jean-Pierre Chevenement to former Socialist foreign minister Claude Cheysson—made their pilgrimages to see Saddam and symbolically offer him a French-style kiss—on both cheeks, of course.

But French misconduct after the first Gulf War may have met its peak in the Oil-for-Food scandal. This refers, of course, to the UN's ambitious humanitarian program that was intended to protect Iraqi citizens from the hardships of the UN-imposed economic sanctions.

Basically, it worked like this: From 1996 to 2003, Iraq was allowed to market limited amounts of its coveted oil, but only under UN supervision. There was one controlling condition: All revenues from the authorized sales would be paid into a UN-controlled escrow account. The United Nations was charged with making sure that any contract Iraq entered into was strictly for food, medicine, or other supplies required for humanitarian needs and not for its army or to enrich its greedy rulers. Once that was ensured, and only then, UN officials released the money from the oil fund to pay for approved Iraqi orders of goods and commodities.

By 2003, $64 billion worth of Iraqi crude oil had been sold under the scheme. Problem was that in addition to approved oil sales, enormous contraband quantities of Iraqi oil were actually sold under the table—much of it through Syria. Moreover, the UN scheme was both corrupt and ineffective. While it helped feed some Iraqi children and improved conditions in some schools and hospitals, millions of other Iraqis and hundreds of Iraqi institutions were left to starve and suffer. Saddam's men systematically withheld distribution of materials in order to make propaganda claims that the UN embargo was killing Iraqi children. Other goons in the Iraqi regime simply hijacked legally imported goods and then sold them privately on the thriving Iraqi black market.

The biggest heist, however, came from the authorized sale of the oil—and France was one of the first in line to share in the profits. While the United Nations did nothing, mountains of money—possibly $21.3 billion—were successfully skimmed by Saddam and his cronies, who built new palaces, filled their Swiss bank accounts, and bought luxuries and weapons systems—while children, schools, and hospitals went without aid. Crooked middlemen in France and elsewhere around the world eagerly shared in the rich profits.

How did Saddam and his friends do it? Under the UN plan,

Iraq was allowed to initially sell its oil to chosen middlemen, who then peddled it on. The ultimate proceeds were supposed to be sent to the UN escrow account. But the prices were set at artificially low levels. And according to reliable accounts, says a lengthy investigative report in the British magazine *The Week,* and later confirmed by U.S. government reports, "when the middlemen went on to sell the oil at a higher price, 10% would be returned in kickbacks. Conversely, those chosen by Baghdad to supply essential goods would wildly overprice the value of shipment, and then channel a chunk of the profits to Saddam."

Saddam's chosen middlemen worked through so-called entitlement vouchers, paper tokens that they sold at huge profits to actual oil traders. In January of 2004, an Iraqi Oil Ministry list of 270 recipients of these vouchers was leaked to the Iraqi press. The names included people and political parties from more than fifty countries, as well as at least three senior UN officials. Most of the names on the list, however, were either Russian or—you guessed it— French. The Gallic Gang reportedly included Charles Pasqua, the former French interior minister (who supposedly held a voucher for twelve million barrels); Jean-Bernard Merimée, the former French ambassador to the United Nations; Father Jean-Marie Benjamin, a French priest at the Vatican who reportedly arranged a much publicized meeting with the pope for Saddam's mouthpiece, then Foreign Minister Tarik Aziz; and Patrick Maugein, an old pal of Jacques Chirac, who reportedly owned Saddam vouchers for more than seventy million barrels of Iraqi oil and has a murky reputation as one of Saddam and Chirac's prime go-betweens.

Many of the same names surfaced in CIA gumshoe Charles Duelfer's October 2004 damning report on Iraq, arms, and oil. Duelfer quotes Tarik Aziz as confirming that French and other individuals who benefited from the shady dealings "understood that resale of the oil was to be reciprocated through efforts to lift UN sanctions, or through opposition to American initiatives within the Security Council." Needless to say, the French nearly blew a gasket when the report surfaced and continue to deny it all. They also refuse to admit that the New York branch of one of France's leading banks, BNP-Paribas, repeatedly violated U.S. money-laundering laws by letting Saddam use its accounts as a financial funnel for his oil-for-food racketeering.

Now let's talk about the vested economic interests France *officially* had in Iraq on the eve of the French-less coalition invasion of Iraq.

In April 2003, while France was doing everything to prevent the toppling of Saddam, Washington's Heritage Foundation compiled an up-to-the-minute catalog list of France's "known" economic interests in Iraq. The details provide ample proof of France's altruistic concern for world peace:

- As of April 1, 2003, France controlled over 22.5 percent of Iraq's imports. French total trade with Saddam Hussein's Iraq under the Oil-for-Food program was the third largest, totaling $3.1 billion since 1996, according to the United Nations.
- In 2001, France became Saddam's largest European trading partner. Roughly sixty French companies did an estimated $1.5

billion in trade with Baghdad in 2001 under the UN Oil-for-Food program.

- France's largest oil company, Total Fina Elf, had negotiated extensive oil contracts to develop the Majnoon and Nahr Umar oil fields in southern Iraq. Both the Majnoon and Nahr Umar fields are estimated to contain as much as 25 percent of the country's oil reserves. The two fields purportedly contain an estimated twenty-six billion barrels of oil. In 2002, the nonwar price per barrel of oil was $25. Based on that average, these two fields have the potential to provide a gross return near $650 billion.

- France's Alcatel company, a major telecom firm, was negotiating a $76 million contract to rehabilitate Iraq's telephone system.

- In 2001, French carmaker Renault SA sold $75 million worth of farming equipment to Iraq.

- More objections had been lodged against French export contracts with Iraq than any other exporting country under the Oil-for-Food program, according to a report published by the London *Times*. In addition, French companies had signed contracts with Saddam's minions worth more than $150 million that were suspected of being linked to its military operations. Some of the goods offered by French companies to Iraq, detailed by UN documents, included refrigerated trucks that could be used as storage facilities and mobile laboratories for biological weapons.

- Saddam owed France an estimated $6 billion in foreign debt accrued from arms sales in the 1970s and 1980s.
- From 1981 to 2001, according to the Stockholm International Peace Research Institute (SIPRI), France was responsible for over 13 percent of Iraq's arms imports.
- Saddam's Iraq still owed France a debt of $10 billion for arms sales prior to Gulf War I.

And this is what we *know* about.

Anyone have any lingering doubts as to why France and Chirac were among those most vehemently opposed to forcibly toppling Saddam?

The hyperbolic UN debate on the second round of war with Iraq made it clear to the American public just how unfaithful the French could be. Asked whom he wanted to win the war, French foreign minister Dominique de Villepin shockingly replied that he didn't know. Polls indicated that at least 33 percent of his countrymen did; they were rooting for Saddam Hussein.

The aftermath of the war that toppled Saddam did little to indicate that beating up on the Yanks was a passing French mood. As one American diplomat put it, "France's anti-Americanism just keeps on reaching new heights."

The French media seemed to especially relish the death of every American or British soldier in Iraq, to focus on every seeming failure of the coalition in Iraq. It was that misanthropic spirit that caused the popular centrist French newsmagazine *l'Express* to title one of its year-end issues: "The Man Who Ruined 2003." The cover picture wasn't of Saddam Hussein or Osama bin Laden—it was of George W. Bush.

The widely read article assailed the American president for what it claimed was his total failure in both Iraq and the War on Terror. All that Bush and the Americans had succeeded in doing, said *l'Express,* was "create worldwide chaos." The article, and similar ones in the French daily press and in television and radio commentary, accused America's "messianic president" of triggering a new spate of terrorist attacks—from Casablanca to Istanbul, from Riyadh to Tokyo.

And who else but the French could possibly shed tears for Saddam Hussein? Soon after U.S. troops pulled the bedraggled ex-dictator out of his spider hole hideaway, a column in the highly influential leftist French daily *Liberation* moaned that it was "shameful" to display Saddam with his long beard and straggly hair—not to mention the indelicacy of showing his teeth being examined and his hair being searched for cooties. The paper, which has had no constraints about showing the mangled bodies of dead American troops, said Washington should get an "Oscar for Bad Taste."

That perhaps should go to the French newsmagazine *Marianne,* which marked the sixtieth anniversary of D-Day with an insulting cover story questioning the propriety of "the Iraq war mongering" George W. Bush, the president of the same United

States that liberated France, attending the memorial ceremonies in Normandy.

And so it goes. France's often duplicitous role in the battle against terrorism and rogue regimes is an increasingly transparent record of fact. Yet irony of ironies, the French continue to assume and even boast of their self-appointed role as Europe's conscience. Fortunately for the rest of us, that posture has begun to sicken even a growing number of their fellow Europeans. British journalist Becky Tinsley recently pointed out that few countries have pursued a less ethical foreign policy, or one more nakedly based on self-interest, than The Proud France.

Writing in the influential *New Statesman,* Tinsley listed with dripping sarcasm all of France's most recent conscience-driven accomplishments, including its lavish arms sales to rogue and totalitarian nations, even its support and aid to the genocidal murderers of Rwanda.

Worse yet, says Tinsley, the French "conscience" is still busy at work in the Balkans where the Quai d'Orsay, the popular name for the French Ministry of Foreign Affairs that is located on that street along the Seine River, "still enjoys a cosy relationship with Serbia"—so cozy that French peacekeeping troops in the region reportedly have allowed Serbian war criminals to move about freely and, according to some sources, even tipped them off about impending arrest attempts.

As for France's much touted love of the *Tiers Monde,* the Third World, Tinsley justifiably accuses the French of being the European Union's "chief defender of the European agricultural subsidies that do untold damage to the developing world."

The French may boast about being the civilized counterweight to "brutal American imperialism," concludes Tinsley, but what they are really doing is "running the cash registers in a Wild West whorehouse."

CHAPTER FIVE

✤ ✤ ✤

Not So Nice in Nice

CULTURE CLASH

Some time ago, I devoted one of my regular op-ed columns in the New York *Daily News* to what I sensed was growing French awareness—and dissatisfaction—with the mounting social, political, and economic problems facing the Fifth Republic.

My American friend Susie Morgenstern, who teaches at the University of Nice, which commands a lovely view of the Mediterranean, told me she'd found the column "so provocative" that she had decided to give it to her English class as a language exercise.

She reported back that my negative, if realistic, views on France had not exactly been received by her students, mostly aged twenty, with great warmth. Well, actually, she said, they were received with great heat; I had become a leading candidate for a campus lynching.

Susie is one of those anomalies in France: an American whom

the French accept as a near equal. A nice Jewish girl from New Jersey, she'd gone to Israel, met a nice Jewish boy from France there, and returned with him to France to settle in Nice. By virtue of her enormous talent, warmth, and sense of humor, she has become a French literary star: In addition to being a popular English *prof,* she is one of France's most popular writers of French-language children's books. Just ask any French kid!

I wanted to find out just what her students really thought about America and suggested that I come to the university for a dialogue cum encounter with them. But the summer break was upon us. Instead, Mme Morgenstern agreed to ask her students to respond to the following questions during a recent end-of-year exam:

1. What is your opinion of America and Americans? Is there a contradiction between French love of American culture and disdain for American values and politics?
2. Many Americans consider the French arrogant. Do you agree?

The answers were deeply revealing, and provided insight into what French educators and media have been feeding their kids. Some were funny, if sarcastic. "I really love America and Americans," wrote twenty-one-year-old Bertrand. "Thanks to them I'll probably soon eat some GMO [genetically modified organisms]. They really bring something new to our poor but well-known culture of junk food. And even if the GMO takes time to come into my house, I'll have the chance to go to one of their famous restaurants called McDonald's where the employees are so patient and so interested in your weight that they help you to become more and more able to survive the cold winter. Indeed, thanks to America we will never know the cold winter again. By rejecting the Kyoto agreement, we may soon even have the chance to swim in the Artic Sea."

Here are some more responses; with only minor editing for space and some language correction, and without actual names.

BLANCHE

I will be sincere. I hate America and Americans. I hate their spirit, I hate their model of life, and mostly I hate their president.

But I must stop being so vindictive. . . . I must be more impartial! There are millions of good Americans and there are also millions of Americans who are controlled by their media and so don't realize what they are doing.

However, "I accuse" [as Émile Zola once said] America of destroying the world. By their mode of life that they export all over the world they are destroying the Earth in the long term. And they also destroy all moral values that existed before: solid family, work. . . . America has imposed a world based on sex and money, a world directed by media . . . a world of great inequality.

Moreover, their nation, which has no history, thinks it can

solve everything even if all the other nations are against them. They think they are superior. When they come to France, they have more disdain in their eyes than admiration for the richness of our society which is the pride of Europe. And they say the French are arrogant!

Nevertheless, we can still all have admiration for those Americans who came to France to deliver us from Nazism.

KEVIN

I'm French and I've always lived in France and it's true that I've never wondered what other people and other countries think of us. I'm a little bit surprised that some qualify us as arrogant. In recent weeks I've welcomed three Americans to my home and none of them ever told me they consider French people arrogant. Maybe some Americans are jealous of the French culture, the French food, the French kiss. . . .

MARC

I hate global opinions. No American is like another American. I'll tell you what I like and don't like. I like the "American Dream" (come to America with nothing in your pocket and live easily). But it is still only a dream.

I dislike the American army, which kills innocent people every day and wages more wars than are necessary; though many Americans react against war. Remember the hippies and the seventies?

I think the worst thing in America is "Wall Street" because its goal is to make money with money. That is an abomination because money is a tool that helps us make exchanges and not a goal!

NATHALIE

Americans and America is something very specific. You have many people in the USA. In my opinion America is good because it has integration and regulations for immigrants are very good. I like the general moralities of American people—but not their values and politics. Many American people agree that their politics are arrogant. American politics injure humans in other countries. Their philosophy is bad: We search for our own advantage and close our eyes to the disadvantage of others.

American politics are to "police" the world. This is not acceptable. It will only impose American ideas on others (look at the problems of pollution and destruction to the ozone atmosphere).

FABIAN

My opinion about America is very mixed. On the one hand, the United States, as it is described in movies, TV series, and books, is the dream place to be: nice weather, beautiful girls, everybody's rich, bad guys always busted. . . . On the other hand, the U.S. lives by one rule: *la loi du plus fort*—the law of the strongest. If you aren't white and rich, you can just get up and start a new life in another country. The lack of social assistance—you have to pay for medical treatment and have no wages when you are retired—makes me think that America is a very hard place to live.

FLORENCE

I think Americans only think about themselves and don't care about the rest of the world. They have to be the best. But that's only the opinion of somebody who never went to the U.S. and never met and had a real conversation with an American. That's only the impression they gave to me particularly when I hear that the American government will not do anything about ecology and the reduction of the emission of gas. But politicians and the people living in the U.S. are not the same at all.

That's why I don't think there is any contradiction between the love we have for American culture and the disdain we have for American values and politics. As for the fact that Americans consider the French arrogant, I agree—though I would have said chauvinistic not arrogant.

ROMAIN

I do really like Americans, especially during these times. The main problem is their way of thinking. They are too stupid! They think because the USA is the most powerful nation in the world, they have all the knowledge in the world, all rights over other people, all rights to decide what is good or not good, all the culture, all the capacity to do whatever they want. And that's the problem: they neglect the rest of the world. They are only guided by the desire to have more and more money. But money should not rule the world.

I would not say that all the French love American culture. Part of the French people are sick of the spread of American culture.

ARMAND

We French are scared of America: its army, politics, agriculture, scientific research, omnipresent police . . . all that is done in America is big, strong, nonflexible, white. And most French have trouble with those concepts. . . . The French suffer from an inferiority complex about Americans. But I think Americans are jerks. It is really terrible to be disgusted by an entire culture, the same one that I adored when I was younger. America evoked for me liberty, technology, and power. Now I just see it as a closed, straight-minded country. The French aren't arrogant. The Americans are just annoyed that we don't adhere to their system and culture.

PATRICIA

If my memory serves me right, America was founded only a few hundred years ago and they are young whereas France exists more than one thousand years. That's a problem. The Americans are jealous of our history and culture and they try to impose their culture of McDonald's and dollars on us. Americans are like children who try to be adults but make big errors as they did in Iraq where all the world knows Bush and his clan have major interests.

CHARLES

It's not only Americans who consider the French arrogant. People in many countries think like that. In my own experience I talked with English, Germans, Belgians, Swiss, Italians, Swedes—and they all say so.

I think in a way they're right. In France we do a lot of exceptional things; some are good and some are bad. We call that *l'Exception Culturelle Française.* We are a very proud people and we like to make fun of other people who don't act like us.

JEAN

I don't really admire America. It's a country where there is a wide gap between people. The poor are totally forgotten by the leadership while rich people have royal living conditions. I can't understand why some social help isn't set up. I'm persuaded it would be possible to reduce the poverty if everybody felt concerned.

Moreover, the war in Iraq didn't help me to admire America. They started the war although they knew they hadn't any reason to justify it. They were only interested in oil, which enables their country to be more and more powerful. They didn't hesitate to use torture on Iraqi soldiers. Every day we discover a new barbarian act.

Regretfully, I must agree that we French are all in love with

American culture. I eat once a week at McDonald's, I drink Coca-Cola, I listen to American music, and I'm astonished by all the American cinematographic super-productions. Besides, it's incredible to see how easily you can make money in the U.S.— far easier than in France. I'm also grateful to the American soldiers who saved the French people in June 1944.

CLAIRE

I'm scared of America: its army, politics, agriculture, scientific research, omnipresent police, prohibition. All of what is done in America is big, strong, nonflexible and most French have trouble with those concepts. They also suffer from an inferiority complex about Americans. But I think that isn't the only reason for hating the USA in general.

My personal disdain for America comes every time I turn on the TV and get into the American clichés that are omnipresent in American TV series.

EDOUARD

Why should two fabulous and developed countries hate each other? America is important for your eyes and France for your mind. But there is a real political problem. Many countries are sickened by the way the USA wants to play world politics in their own interest (oil, dollars . . .). The United States is the only country that can declare war on another for bad reasons and against United Nations agreements. How could the world improve if the U.S. sparks riots and war whenever they want for monetary gain instead of bridging the gap between the Third World and us? With so much power they could make so many things better in this dark world.

There is a contradiction between French love of American culture and disdain for American values and politics. For English and Americans we will forever be "The Frog Eaters." And probably we are seen as arrogant because we are an old country with rich culture and a long history.

CHAPTER SIX

✤ ✤ ✤

Frère Jacques, Dormez-Vous?

"La Belle France"

No one has been spotted sharpening guillotine blades, but we may be witnessing the onset of another French Revolution. Slowly, but very surely, there are those among the French who are beginning to figure out what most everyone else has known for years: La Belle France ain't so *belle* anymore.

There's no denying, President Jacques Chirac and his merry band of musketeers still swagger ad nauseum about the glory of *La République* and the righteousness of its "independent" (read: anti-American) foreign policy. But some of those among the French public who bother to read the world press and/or check out the national economic statistics—not to mention their monthly bank statements—see little but gloom staring them in the face. Even Mont Blanc, France and Europe's tallest mountain, has shrunk— by four meters according to latest measurements of its shrinking ice cap (must be that American-generated earth warming).

In fact, for all its arrogant posturing, says French writer Nicolas Baverez, today's France is wallowing in "economic, political and social stagnation."

Baverez is the author of a 2003 best-seller called *France Is Falling Down* and one of a new breed of French doomsday prophets, most of them historians, who have recently published similar "cassandratic" tomes about the current state of France and the dismal future it faces unless it seriously mends its ways. In addition to Baverez's book, there is *Adieu to a Departing France* by Jean-Marie Rouart, *French Disarray* by Alain Duhamel, and *French Arrogance* by Romain Gubert and Emmanuel Saint-Martin.

When these new French reality books first began to appear last year, they quickly became hot topics of conversation from Normandy to the Riviera.

Charles de Gaulle once complained that it was impossible to govern a country with 246 varieties of *fromage*. In fact, there are closer to 500 varieties. And as Baverez and his colleagues see it, there may be more problems in France than there are varieties of cheese. They range from economic to social to cultural. Moreover, France's membership in the European Community may be adding to the woes rather than helping to solve them.

The European Union's internal open-border system is certainly adding to the influx of immigrants to France from poorer countries, a phenomenon with which, in the past, France has been able to successfully cope by integrating newcomers into the life of the Republic. Today, that is becoming more and more difficult to do.

Differences between rich and poor are growing not diminishing, the cost of living is rising, and a generation of idle youth are resentful of having been excluded from the economic life of France—all have provoked an institutional crisis that challenges the foundation of French society. Overt racism and anti-Semitism are back. There is an ever-increasing influence of radical Islamism in the urban and suburban ghettos, a surge of violence in the streets, the recrudescence of hate literature spread through the Web, the fear of unemployment in an economy that has remained stagnant for many years, and a political leadership that undertakes reforms in homeopathic dribbles rather than with heavy doses of economic antibiotics. "All of these problems," says one political observer, "throw the Republican ideal into question."

Consider the following: Just last year, this nation of sixty million people had more bankruptcies than the entire United States with its more than two hundred million people. France's current national unemployment rate still hovers at double digits. The numbers on welfare are growing not diminishing. Meanwhile, a recent study by the World Economic Forum ranks France only twenty-sixth in the league of growth markets—behind Portugal. According to Baverez, the French failure to truly liberalize its economy by loosening its bureaucratic straitjacket, has caused new-business creation to drop in France by 2 percent a year since the late 1980s.

As if all that weren't bad enough, French economic life continues to be regularly paralyzed by surges in strike action by people who think social benefits grow on the grapevines of Bordeaux and Burgundy. France, says Baverez, is becoming "an industrial and entrepreneurial desert."

There are those who argue that all is not disaster—and all is certainly not. "France is still the fifth-richest country in the world," points out TV journalist Christine Ockrent. "And for all the moaning and groaning, it's still a marvelous place to live."

Indeed, while its self-perception may be as overinflated as a super *soufflé,* France is not without modern accomplishments. Among the world's few real nuclear powers, it still boasts one of the world's largest economies.

It has also been in the avant-garde of some of our high-tech age's most ingenious achievements. France was among the first nations to incorporate microchips into credit and bank cards. And a full decade before Americans became as computerized and plugged into the Internet as we are, France Telecom, the French equivalent of our old Ma Bell, had developed the Minitel system, handing out free mini-screen computers that enabled French phone users to tap in through their home or office phone line and check bank accounts, book airline tickets, or even find love matches for an afternoon *rendez-vous.*

Even now, France's aircraft industry produces ever bigger and better versions of its already internationally successful Airbus—a joint project of France, Italy, the United Kingdom, Germany, and Spain. And for popular luxury and speed there's little that can match France's 180-mile-per-hour superspeed trains, the slick

TGV (*Trains de Grand Vitesse*), which can whip you in great comfort from Marseille to Paris (411 miles) in less than three hours.

Problem is, many of these modern wonders have run their course—or are simply proving too costly. Though largely passé, Minitel is still widely in use. Yet by counterpoint, French households boast far fewer home computers per capita than America does. More to the point, France Telecom has a mountain of national debt that now exceeds a staggering $15 billion (not all because of Minitel), and the French government has been forced to sell a growing percentage of its shares in the company.

Other national sources of pride manage to survive only with fat subsidies the French government can ill afford. Everyone adores the ever-expanding TGV system, but SNCF, France's national train company, has a nightmarish multibillion-euro debt—and so far, the prospect for TGV becoming economically sound are as good as the defunct Concorde's was.

One result of all the problems: Economic growth has ground to a near halt. Even new socioeconomic ideas are proving a disaster. A revolutionary French move to a thirty-five-hour workweek was supposed to generate new jobs and give workers more free time. Instead, it has screwed up production and made those with jobs poorer—and ended up with workers complaining about unrealistic quotas. Now the government is finding it tough to convince workers to return to the old system of a full week's work even though it would still give most French workers an average of five full weeks a year of paid vacation.

"It's completely crazy," says French parliamentarian Pierre Lellouche. "It's an escapism—to be in a country where they seriously discuss a thirty-five-hour workweek and have a government that can't tell people realities."

Critics of the government blame Jacques Chirac's Union Pour un Mouvement Populaire (UMP) for the lack of reality. "The point is that the leading right-wing party can't say it," says Lellouche. "Partly because the leadership of the party is weak and cowardly and incompetent. But it's also because they know they can't win an election by becoming [productive like the] Chinese—Europeans don't want to work that hard! . . . We are an exhausted society, exhausted with history and war, we have no ambition."

They also don't seem to have much willingness to do a day's work. Despite the flagging economy, fewer and fewer people in France appear prepared to work at all. Indeed, while those who do work have a notably high level of productivity, there's a growing problem in France of laziness. A rising percentage of the population relies on full or partial national welfare programs. And attempts at cutting back on welfare benefits for the unemployed meet with stiff and raucous opposition. Who else but the French would have a labor union of the unemployed?

Of those who do work, few fully understand or care about the concept of service. Of course, service was never a big item in France, except for that part of the bill that forms a tip. For example, try ordering a simple lunch at a café before twelve noon or after two P.M. Or attempt to ask for a variation of an item on the menu.

The first answer is inevitably *"Non,"* or a denial of responsibility. The second is to fall back on Cartesian logic. One friend of mine recently purchased a brand-new Renault only to soon run into problems with the car's starter—sometimes it worked, sometimes it didn't. The authorized garage she consulted refused to even look at it. Under the warranty, explained the chief mechanic, the starter was covered only for "full breakdown," not occasional breakdown. He did give her a twenty-four-hour phone number to call if it did fully break down, which it did. The twenty-four-hour number didn't answer.

Indolence is also on the rise. Increasing numbers of French workers try to find ways to loaf on the job. Small wonder that one of France's biggest best-sellers this past summer was a book called *Bonjour Paresse,* Hello Laziness, a sort of Slacker's Guide to Sloth.

The author is a well-educated forty-year-old bureaucrat named Corinne Maier. She earns $2,000 a month writing boring economic reports for Electricité de France, the state-run French electric utility. Angered by France's fossilized corporate culture and the little chance of advancement it offers, she decided to encourage her colleagues in France's workforce to join her in a system of "active disengagement"—or more to the point, calculated loafing (e.g., "do little, but look busy, always carry a stack of files").

"French corporations are not meritocracies," she recently complained to an interviewer. "Everything depends on what school you went to and what diploma you have . . . why not spread gangrene through the system from inside?"

One of the few things the French seem always eager to work at is finding new ways to go on holiday. Used to be that you could get nothing done during the month of August—the dentist was gone, the dry cleaner was closed, and forget about an electrician. Then they staggered holidays between July and August. Now you can't get much done either month (even swimming pool repairmen take holidays in the French summertime).

They're even talking about the right to increased, not less, leisure—a rather delusional concept in a nation whose social welfare coffers are already dangerously hemorrhaging. But most French still fail to see it as delusionary; they just won't believe the train is heading for a crash. As far as the French are concerned, working less and enjoying life more, having longer weekends and monthlong holidays, is a legitimate objective of society. "We want to be a society in which we enjoy life," says Parisian business executive Claude Sentier. "If you are a Baltic state or Poland you are more hungry than the others, so you work harder, you emulate the American work ethic—but that doesn't work in France."

Indeed, the French, even more than other European social economies, says parliamentarian Lellouche, "believe the state should take care of their lives, take care of our children, our old people. Being 'taken care of' has become a religion here . . . they don't want to see that there are people hungrier than they are, and therefore willing to work harder. . . . I'm worried for my children."

And he should be. As more and more French critics see it, there is a growing loss of the work ethic, a breakdown of the economy, and a split in the culture. The result: The very idea of the French Republic—secular, democratic, and the embodiment of universal values—is increasingly being challenged by rapidly changing social and political realities . . . and by a lowering of standards. The political class, as almost everywhere in Europe, is criticized as being out of touch with the lives of ordinary people.

"The distance between what observers in the past called institutional France and ordinary society is becoming a virtually unbridgable gap," says Norman Roseman. "People shrug their shoulders and turn their back on the political world. Rarely has France been so fragile or the hard-won effort to create a Republic for all men so threatened."

A few French officials recognize the problems and even speak out. "France is not great when it is arrogant," Foreign Minister Michel Barnier warned a recent conference of French diplomats. "It is not strong if it is alone."

Unfortunately, not enough of his ambassadors were listening.

France is also finding the challenge of the European Union a tough one to meet. Though French statesmen such as Jean Monnet pioneered the very concept of a Europe united as one, the idea is proving easier for the French political mentality than the reality—especially with the twenty-five-member union now expanded to include East European nations that are far more pro-American than they are pro-French.

"France is right to be scared, especially when a group of newcomers thinks that the route to their security lies with the U.S.," says Polish politician Jan Rokita, the man who's sometimes touted as his country's future prime minister. According to Rokita, leader of the Polish center-right Civic Platform Party, France sees the entry of East European countries to the E.U. as nothing less than a threat to its "monopoly over Europe."

Relations with the newcomers reached a low in 2003 when Jacques Chirac attacked Central and Eastern European countries—including Poland—for supporting American policy in Iraq. Scolding them as though they were misguided children, Chirac publicly declared that they'd "missed an opportunity to keep quiet."

Complains Rokita: France does not believe it is "just one of the centers of Europe. They believe that they are the leaders of Europe and that everybody should recognize this." The entry of East European countries who don't think that way is seen by the French as a threat to their "monopoly over Europe."

There are some who argue that, in fact, France has given up the pretension of being Europe's most important leader. "France will be a major factor in the European Union because it has already agreed to give up many levels of power to the E.U.," says

Paris attorney Mark Cohen, a legal adviser to one of France's largest corporations.

But France is also finding it increasingly difficult to keep up with some of the E.U.'s basic economic standards. For three straight years France has broken the European Commission's national deficit cap of 3 percent—and firmly resisted E.U. demands for any more budget cuts. Asked to carry out a structural deficit reduction in 2005 of just 1 percentage point, France at first haughtily rejected the request, arguing that six billion euros in savings would "destabilize" the budget and jeapordize France's fragile economy. The appointment in 2004 of pragmatic Nicolas Sarkozy as minister of finance seemed to reverse that refusal.

It remains to be seen whether he can. For what France does not say is that its government has always lacked the political will to overhaul France's budget because its population lacks the will to accept any social sacrifices to do so. The very idea of cutbacks in ill-afforded social benefits is enough to bring thousands of drum-beating, banner-waving French strikers out into the streets of every major city in the country. Unlike the United States, writes Baverez, French leaders believe "the more things change, the more must be done to change nothing."

What has changed dramatically is the face of France. That has resulted from a massive flow of immigration from Islamic, African, and Asian countries. French society's inability to deal with that demographic upheaval is certainly not the sole cause of its current sad state, but it is very much part of the problem. The prestigious *Le Monde* calls it the "problem of two Frances."

Immigration is not new to France. For generations, the republic successfully and willingly absorbed waves of economic and political immigrants—Poles, Jews, Russians, Italians, Spaniards, and Portuguese. All the while it remained uniquely French. Even twenty years ago, more than one-third of the French population counted at least one foreign-born grandparent.

Most of those newcomers successfully integrated into French life. Even if they preserved some of their ethnic and religious traditions, they were prepared to accept the monolithic French culture that France insists comes before individual ethnic and religious identities. Far fewer of the millions of migrants who have flooded into France from the Third World over the past generation have been willing or able to do the same. Many of those in this Second France were encouraged to come to the mainland from France's North African colonies—Tunis, Algeria, and Morocco—during the 1950s and 1960s. They would do the dirty manual labor that postwar Frenchmen weren't interested in doing. Many brought their families. Most never returned.

More than 10 percent of the French population is now what the French pejoratively call *Arabe*. A tense cultural divide has developed that grows worse, not better. When I first lived in France almost forty years ago, new immigrants from North Africa spoke Maghreb Arabic. Their children, however, quickly learned and eagerly spoke French, even among themselves. That has changed.

Rejected socially, culturally, and economically by much of "French France," North African immigrants have become increasingly defensive of their own separate ghettolike culture. Walk in any French city today, and you will hear *beurs,* the young French-born generation of Maghrebians speaking to one another in Arabic, not French.

All the same, France's cultural elite continues to resist embracing the creative energy bursting from French artists, writers, and performers of African, Arab, and Asian descent. "The energy is certainly there," noted the *New York Times,* "in stand-up comedians and above all in pop music, the art form where performers and public can most readily connect without the mediation of cultural institutions."

But in theater, movies, television, and the visual arts, this "other France" is far less visible. There is a near-absence of black or Arab anchors on French television. "Should television exclude people only because the color of their skin and their name are different?" asks Zair Kedadouche, a French-Arab politician.

The problem is similar to the French fear of foreign words in their language. More than most, the French view their culture as their identity. And there is sharp but clear separation of religion and secular life in the French republican system—hence the ban on the wearing of head scarves in public schools by Muslim girls (and excessively large crosses by Christians or skullcaps by Jews).

Many worry about demography. "One out of every three babies born in France today is a Muslim baby," claims one populist

French blogger. "And that means, in twenty years, one of every three twenty-year-olds in France will be a Muslim twenty-year-old. And that means, twenty years after that, at present rates of reproduction, France will have a majority Muslim population. Where shall we hide . . . the Venus de Milo?"

Indeed, France's Muslim minority seems increasingly alienated, and there's been a resurgence of scapegoat attacks on its Jewish minority, mostly by members of the Muslim community, who, ironically, like the Jews, are themselves victims of persecution and bigotry by the people Jacques Chirac dangerously refers to as "simple Frenchmen"—a reference that grates because it implies that French Jews and French Muslims are somehow not completely French.

All together, urban crime, once defined by the French as strictly an American phenomenon, is on a rapid rise. In fact, violence in France has become so bad that magistrates recently demanded extra security in their courtrooms, and witnesses frequently refuse to testify for fear of retribution from housing project hoods.

The nation also continues to be wracked by governmental and corporate corruption—a corruption so widespread that, as Paris lawyer Marc Cohen puts it, "most French simply feel it's a fact of life that can't be corrected." Some of the most notorious cases involve President Jacques Chirac himself. Alain Juppé, Chirac's right-hand man and heir apparent, was banned from office for a decade after being found guilty of illegal party financing—a political scandal that assumed the proportions of a Watergate *à la française.*

But Juppé, a former prime minister and current mayor of Bordeaux, quickly broke his promise to resign if found guilty by taking advantage of a law that allowed him to stay in office pending appeal. "Who hasn't made mistakes?" he asked an audience of thirteen million viewers on French television, noting that every party in France had been guilty of the same crime for at least the past twenty years.

Juppé's crime—he put seven party officials on the Paris city-hall payroll—is believed be the tip of a much larger payment iceberg set afloat by Chirac while he was mayor of the French capital. Reportedly, the scam involved forcing construction companies to pay secret kickbacks for public contracts. *Le Nouvel Observateur*, the French leftist weekly, gleefully noted that Chirac, who is untouchable while in office, is named in nine current investigations for corruption.

Even France's most cherished social institutions are in disrepute. After years of boasting the world's best health care system, fifteen thousand old people died in a heat wave the summer of 2003 . . . because it wasn't. Adding insult to injury, France is now asking workers to give up one vacation day a year to pay for improvements—and has been meeting with stiff resistance from unions.

Baverez and the other doomsayers claim that without radical shock therapy France's future is doomed. They point to a disastrous brain drain: 265,000 of France's best and brightest have packed up and left over the last decade—doctors, engineers, scientists. As for France's military, it's now considered by many to be a joke—60 percent of its helicopters, 50 percent of the navy's ships, and 75 percent of its light troop carriers reportedly don't work—and its influence and significance abroad is mostly impotent posturing. In *French Arrogance,* journalists Romain Gubert and Emmanuel Saint-Martin argue that France looks silly because of its "sermons" and "empty gestures," especially over Iraq. "This obsession about status, the hatred of decline, the worry about grandeur: these are the guiding principles of French foreign policy," say Gubert and Saint-Martin. "But when there aren't the means to back it up, it's just ridiculous!"

Even French culture has seen better days. France may still boast the world's finest collections of Renoir and Toulouse-Lautrec, but these days more innovation can be found in the art worlds of New York, London, and Berlin than in those of Paris. Pop culture is also in the doldrums. Instead of Yves Montand, Edith Piaf, Georges Brassens, and Jean Sablon (my late mother's favorite), the best the French can offer are bad copies of Britney Spears and that aging poor-man's Elvis, Johnny Halliday.

To be fair, there are still occasional French film triumphs. But for the most part, French cinemas rely on Hollywood fare (most especially Michael P. Moore). As for French television, it's overwhelmed by U.S. sit-coms and dramas dubbed in French (French TV's "Le West Wing" doesn't refer to the Élysée Palace).

Threatened, too, are France's beloved educational standards. Paris is no longer the intellectual capital of the world. And while the French *Grandes Ecoles* still maintain their standards, mainstream French universities continue in what has been a long-term decline. Because most colleges are banned from selecting pupils on the basis of ability and instead have open-door policies for all high school graduates, they suffer from huge dropout rates. France's brightest students try to head across the Atlantic, or sign up for the branches of small American business universities that have sprung up across the continent. To the embarassment of the French, mainstream universities suffer from up to 90 percent annual exam failure rates.

"The price of our failure to reform is there for all to see," says a leading academic, "though most would rather avert their gaze. Graduates of Europe's universities once won 75 percent of the Nobel prizes; American graduates garnered 25 percent. Now the figures are reversed, indicating that Europe's academic decline has been even more precipitous than its economic decline."

And woe is me—and anybody else who considers themselves a big-time *gourmand* —even that fabled wonder of French culture, *la cuisine,* has fallen on hard times. "Our 30 years of glory are over," Parisian restaurateur Jean-Claude Vrinat, owner of the Michelin three-star Taillevent, recently moaned in an *International Herald Tribune* article titled "The Crisis in French Cookery."

To France's great chagrin, London and New York chefs now easily compete with the best in France. And while you may still occasionally partake in Paris, Lyon, or the countryside of one of those culinary feasts of yore that will lift you out of your seat with heavenly taste delights, the once common experience is becoming rare and rarer—while the prices grow high and higher.

A shocking number of restaurants have even forsaken the fresh preparation of food—something that was a near capital crime thirty years ago. Instead, they are serving their disappointed clients microwave-heated, even prepackaged meals. *Mon Dieu,* it's enough to make Escoffier and the other grand masters of French culinary art spin in their graves. It's certainly a far cry from the days of Louis XIV, whose great chef Vatel is reputed to have killed himself because the fresh fish he planned to serve the Sun King arrived at his kitchen too late for dinner.

Want to really weep? That once marvelous French home cooking has taken a twenty-first-century hit. In today's France, it's increasingly more likely that *Maman* will serve up frozen fish sticks and canned string beans rather than fresh sole meunière and farm-fresh haricots.

Need proof? Just visit any of the ever-growing chain of French *super-marchés.* Time was most French shopped by the day in the open-air market or at quaint local butcher, baker, and vegetable shops—fresh bread in the morning, enough meat, fresh vegetables, and fruit for a day, maximum two.

Today, long lines of French shoppers ring up increasingly large piles of frozen and prepared food at supermarket cash registers, including a growing array of American-style junk foods with names like Artic-cool and Kwik-choco. One result: The French, who have always laughed at the obesity of Americans, are now facing a growing problem of their own overweight, especially among children. I would give them odds at any international keester contest.

Alors, what to do? In *Adieu to a Departing France,* novelist Jean-Marie Rouart, a member of the august Academie Française, says that France is losing its soul to mediocrity and needs a great de Gaulle–like leader to restore its grandeur.

Some French pundits—both Left and Right—look toward personalities like Nicolas Sarkozy, now France's dynamic young president of the UMP party, who has already indicated he plans to challenge Jacques Chirac and his old guard and offer France a vision of change and a healthier attitude toward America.

The conservative French—Left, Right, and Center—fearful of change and comfortable with a status quo, no matter how destructive it is, may stick with what's familiar. Still other French voters continue to see solutions to France's woes in the facist nightmare offered by extreme right-wing demagogues like Jean-Marie Le Pen. In the first round of the last presidential race, this French Mussolini actually came in second with a full 24 percent of the national vote.

He was soundly defeated in the second round, but Le Pen and his ilk cannot be ruled out as politically dead in future pollings. Commentator Alain Duhamel, another leading declinist, argues in his book *French Disarray* that the malaise is so deep, French democracy itself is at stake.

CHAPTER SEVEN

✤ ✤ ✤

Some of My Best Friends . . .

AS A SON of A SON of FRENCH IMMIGRANTS IT IS WITH A MIX OF SHAME AND EMBARRASSMENT THAT I SEE THE FRENCH ACTING SO VERY, WELL, FRENCH. LIKE MANY IMMIGRANT FAMILIES WE WERE IMBUED WITH A DEEP SENSE OF GRATITUDE FOR THIS COUNTRY. WHILE AT THE SAME TIME LOOKING WISTFULLY OVER OUR SHOULDERS BACK AT THE MOTHER COUNTRY. SO THE GROWING FEELINGS OF ANTI-FRANCOPHILIA ARE DISHEARTENING. NOT TO MENTION COMPLETELY WARRANTED.

WE GAVE ZAT TO THEM, YOU KNOW

FRENCH LIKE ME
by Scott Stantis

GROWING UP IN A FAMILY WHERE FRENCH WAS OFTEN THE FIRST LANGUAGE WASN'T SO BAD. IN THE LAND OF STEREOTYPES FRENCH-AMERICANS GOT OFF EASY WITH THE OCCASIONAL "FROG", I MEAN, WE WERE SO FAR OFF THE CULTURAL RADAR THAT THE HIGHEST PROFILE FRENCH-AMERICAN WHEN I WAS GROWING UP WAS PEPE LE PEW.

RIDDING THE WORLD OF DESPOTS SEEMS TO ME A NOBLE UNDERTAKING. IRAQ IS A GOOD PLACE TO START.

I DON'T GET IT. THE ONLY REASON I CAN FIGURE THAT THE FRENCH LIKE SADDAM SO MUCH IS BECAUSE HE, TOO, IS PARTIAL TO BERETS..

FRENCH PRESIDENT JACQUES CHIRAC MADE MATTERS WORSE WHEN, AT THE LATEST NATO MEETING, HE PITCHED WHAT MANY LEARNED FOREIGN POLICY EXPERTS HAVE TERMED "UNE GRANDE HISSY FIT." CONFIRMING TO THE WORLD THAT ALL CHILDREN OF GAUL ARE GENETICALLY PREDISPOSED TO ACT LIKE FRENCH WAITERS.

SO NOW THE FLOOD GATES OF ETHNIC BILE ARE OPEN WIDE. SPEWING ANTI-FRENCH JOKES ON THE RADIO, LENO and LETTERMAN, NEWSPAPERS AND THE INTERNET. (I GET THEM E-MAILED TO ME ALMOST DAILY.) THERE ARE CALLS FOR BOYCOTTS OF FRENCH PRODUCTS. EVEN CHANGING THE NAME OF FRENCH FRIES. BUT IN THE RUSH TO INSULT, DEMEAN AND BOYCOTT WE RUN THE RISK OF BECOMING.....FRENCH.

EVEN WITH ALL OF THIS I AM PROUD TO BE FRENCH...

..I'M JUST PROUDER TO BE AN AMERICAN.

STANTIS ©2003 USA TODAY

So, you may ask, why in the world do you live there?

Why indeed?

Recently I sat in a small but popular local café complaining in French to some friends about a nasty anti-American article in the influential daily *Le Monde* and moaning in general about France's misanthropic view of life.

"Monsieur," asked a gentleman whom I'd never seen before and who was sitting at a nearby table, "if things are so bad in France, why do you stay here?"

"Ahh, Monsieur," I replied, "because you have great wine, wonderful cheese, and remarkably beautiful women."

He laughed approvingly, and we all clicked glasses of cool Côtes du Rhône wine.

Simplistic, cavalier, hedonistic, and decidedly shallow—but there's a lot to it. I am not, as one of my friends insists, turning into another bubbling Francophile determined to add to the popular American myth that the French countryside is paradise on earth. I know France's drawbacks—rural and urban—and I recognize the frustrations the French represent. Yet despite all its many faults, despite Descartes, despite its lousy international policies, despite the moods, the pretensions, and the bad attitudes, after a lifetime lived overseas I personally find the quality of my day-to-day life in France far superior to anything that I could afford back home in the U.S.A.

That doesn't mean that I don't thoroughly enjoy my three to four months a year back in the United States, recharging my cultural batteries with theater, concerts, opera, and American humor—not to mention authentic hamburgers. Nor does it mean that the rest of the year I don't miss the open debate, freewheeling conversation, and warmth of true, easygoing friendship that is so uniquely American.

Yet once back in my French country home, I have the serenity that I, personally, have never been able to find in any American city, the sophistication that I have never found in the American countryside—though it may exist there. I also have the constant presence of that special natural beauty and ageless time that I regularly discover and rediscover in the cream-colored stone walls of my medieval village and in the higgledy-piggledy farmhouses— renovated or *à la nature*—that cling to its hills. I like the sound of farmers' tractors in the early morning, the yellow and green Van Gogh–like fields of sunflowers in the early summer, the melancholy red colors of the vineyards in early fall, the year-round pride the market vendors take in the quality of their rich-tasting home-grown tomatoes and apricots; freshly caught Mediterranean fish; in-the-basket displays of twenty-seven varieties of olives—green, black, and multicolor; the multichoice of farm cheeses; and that unequaled-anywhere smell and taste of freshly baked French breads. The bereted peasant biking past my window with a baguette of bread tucked under his arm . . .

Okay, I admit that's the postcard view! The reality is far from that mythological paradise known as the French countryside, the view painted by generations of American romantics. The French are beginning to build ugly cement-block houses on the edge of beautiful villages. The noise of tractors at four A.M. can be more than bothersome. Many of the veggies and fruits and other meats, fish, and products now come from Spain or Morocco or even Chile. And the farmer often buys his bread in the *super-marché*.

But there's more to France than postcard views. For all its maddening modern failings, for all its whining pretensions, the true France remains rich in historic creation and in a nobility of spirit that continues to enthrall those who come in contact with it. This is still a land aglow with valuable tradition—tradition that many French still cling to and generously share with those in their midst.

That said, let me hasten to add that you have to separate the wheat from the constant bologna, to overmix a metaphor. Nor do any of those formidable virtues of the previous paragraph give

France the right to deserve anywhere near the premier leadership role it demands in today's modern world. The bottom line is simple: France's glorious history gives it as much right to pass solemn judgment on modern world events as say modern Greece might claim because of its past glories.

I also try to remind myself that there was a time when France's brightest minds viewed America not as an imperialistic threat but as the incarnation of Reason and Liberty, our republican democracy as the ultimate realization of the Enlightment, the hope of social justice.

It was during those heady days, immediately after the start of the French Revolution, that the General Marquis de Lafayette, among the first Frenchmen to rally to the American Revolutionary cause, joined forces with his friend Thomas Jefferson, the American minister to Paris. By light of candles (and one supposes with a good bottle of Bordeaux at their side) they jointly drew up a European Declaration of Rights based upon the same principles of inalienable rights and liberties that Jefferson had drafted for the thirteen colonies. Their document was unanimously adopted by the new French Assembly and was soon being read aloud in villages all across France.

We've wandered along a curving path of antagonism and occasional friendships since then. But never has French animosity toward America been at such feverish heights as it has been during the presidency of the man the French have come to call "Le

Cowboy"—George W. Bush. Ignoring American political realities—and our own sometimes demeaning attitude toward Europe—the French were convinced that a Democratic victory would alter what the French perceive as America's new push for hegemony.

Writing in the *Wall Street Journal* before the presidential elections, Jean-Marie Colombani, editor of *Le Monde,* noted: "Today, 'containment' has given way to 'pre-emptive war'; and the logic of development and free-trade threatens to be replaced by a return of protectionism. In our interdependent and already multi-polar world, the two main axes being wielded by Mr. Bush (as opposed to his father) are therefore a threat to the very foundation of the historical alliance between the U.S. and Europe. This is why John Kerry is, *a priori,* perceived with so much sympathy. He personifies the promise of an America that will get back on track—more just, more cohesive, more generous. In brief, less 'unilateral.' So that we can still all remain 'American' in years to come."

The reply came from American analyst John Vinocur in a preelectoral commentary from Washington: "Wide segments of [French] opinion, official and public, confidential or boisterous, want Bush beaten. Many influential Europeans seem to believe that Senator John Kerry in a Democratic White House would restore both respectful equanimity to the American side of the trans-Atlantic relationship and, perhaps more naïvely, aim to redefine U.S. interests in a way that did not seem so self-interestedly American.

"Pushed to the extreme, this might be called the European School for Reforming America. In this notion, a needy United States seeks out European counsel, converts to multilateralism and submits get-tough inclinations to the United Nations for the veto-ready muster of China, Russia and France."

Fact is, that while John Kerry may speak French and even have a cousin or two somewhere in Brittany, even most Democrats remain only mildly interested in Europe's, and specifically France's, view on world policy. And therein may lie not a solution to the problem but at least the first steps toward a closing of the growing gap: a sincere display of American interest—Republican and Democrat—in French and European opinions. Not a solution, not a call for America to curry to the pompous of Euro-opinion, nor to abandon our own commitments, but an attempt to assuage France's sense of being totally dismissed by the world's only true superpower.

"The worst fate the French can imagine is to be ignored," says American journalist Robert Lane Greene. The remedy for that may be a matter of involving France—not patronizingly but in a way that says to the French we are interested in what you think, though we may neither agree with it nor follow your advice.

And some improvements are possible. Toward that end, French-American affairs expert Dominique Moisi suggests the establishment of a "council of wise men to examine what's wrong in our relationship and how to improve it." Several French parliamentarians have proposed a high-level Franco-American conference to work out common strategies. "It doesn't mean common interests will be reconciled," says Pierre Lellouche, "but it will be a start. Perhaps," he adds with a smile, "we can meet in [the French West Indies island of] Martinique—that would please the French."

New York financier and former U.S. ambassador to France Felix Rohatyn suggests that "the New America" turn toward greater cooperation with the "New Europe," which for all its cumbersome twenty-five-nation size, he believes will ultimately be led by a triumvirate of Britain, Germany, and France.

Such renewed sensitivity to our French friends and their neighbors may not return us to the days when Tin Pan Alley sheet music featured General Black Jack Pershing and Marshal Ferdinand Foch reaching out to one another across the Atlantic. But it may help the Marquis de Lafayette rest more quietly in his grave and help France to wake up to its own realities, forget its obsession with America, and heal itself.

Finally, I take odd heart in one bizarre aspect of French culture: the national fascination with the absurd.

For all its devotion to lost grandeur, for all its smothering educational system, for all the Cartesian rationalism shoved down their throats as though they were geese force-fed to produce swollen livers for foie gras, the French secretly recoil from the rational. "The French have traditionally taken a gutsy delight in the irrational all the way to the absurd," says Paris psychotherapist Brenda Foguel. "They love the antihero."

Alfred Jarry, the nineteenth-century creator of France's classic literary buffoon Ubu Roi, once wrote that "the absurd exercises the mind and makes the memory work." In the case of the French, says Foguel, it possibly takes them "back to fantasies that help combat fearful shivers of inadequacy and failure."

And who are the favorite antiheroes of the French? More often than not American. Where else in the world is Jerry Lewis's jerky pratfall comedy still considered absolute stand-on-your-feet-and-cheer genius? Want to see a truly long line for the movies, check the next showing on the Champs Élysées of any new film by classic New York shlub Woody Allen. Both Lewis and Allen, like Charlie (Charlot) Chaplin before them, are sacred icons of French culture whose only current rival may be documentary propagandist Michael P. Moore—an antihero if there ever was one.

How did these Yanks get to the top of the French pops? One school of thought suggests that it is precisely because they represent the antithesis of how the French perceive their archrival Americans: the tough cowboy hero, the Rambo figure that today's French culture fears and rejects. The antihero is the non-American American. His humiliating slides on banana peels provide a way of freely laughing at Yankee foibles.

It may be far more than that. Antiheroes, says psychotherapist Foguel, express the real but unmentionable side of life for the French, their own humiliating, strictly forbidden slides on the banana peel, their secret devotion to the art of living with the irrational, their hidden desire to feel sometimes less than heroic without feeling guilty about it.

Perhaps we Americans say something openly that the French can acknowledge only in the darkness of their cinemas: Don't always take yourself so seriously. Would that the French take off their Cartesian girdles in the sunlight, recognize their shortcomings and growing national problems, and finally do something about them.

When that day comes, the French perception of France will start to mature. Instead of *Plus ça change, plus c'est la même chose*—the more things change, the more they stay the same—France's most popular saying might become: The more things change, the more there's a chance to improve.

When that happens, France will be bound to feel better about itself. When France does that, then the nation we once considered our oldest ally may feel better about America and that alliance.

✠ ✠ ✠

How to Respond
to Rude French People

Here is some advice for anyone considering a trip to France: You must come well prepared. I'm not just talking about your passport, endless supplies of euros, and at least one bag of your favorite chocolate chip cookies. I'm talking about arriving with the means to defend yourself against the French. This is certainly the case for Americans.

Mace, fists, and/or brass knuckles (known as a *poing americain*) are strongly frowned on by French authorities. But responding verbally to someone who has been insulting, offensive, or simply ignored you is considered a legitimate defense under French law—as long as you don't use racist or sexist terms.

Reacting to insult may not be considered very chic in some French circles. "It's much more dignified simply to ignore ill-mannered people," says one hoity-toity Parisian acquaintance of mine. Another friend warns that responding to an insult by counterinsulting may cause an unwanted escalation from which there is no backing down.

In my experience, responding to insult in France may not be considered best form, but it is respected, and you may find that in the finest of French traditions, the offender may simply back off. Even if your French is the heavily accented relic of some high school or college course of long times past, or even if you don't speak French at all, you can arm yourself with some choice expressions of rejoinder. Unfortunately, the most common French ones are decidedly foul and either sexually insulting or scatological in nature—the sort of category of turn of phrase most recently enshrined in our national political scene by Vice President Dick Cheney and Teresa Heinz Kerry.

There are, however, some French repartees that are more or less proper, and even considered by the French to be rather *rafinée*. You probably won't find them in your electronic English-French dictionary. But if you memorize them and employ them at precisely the right moment, you may yet have the last word! It's not a guarantee you'll win the war, but you will have the satisfying experience of battle victory.

Let's say you have arrived in Paris, or Marseille, or some tiny French village in between and you want to check into your hotel or charming *auberge*. You've been on an overnight red-eye flight from the States, the unloading of the baggage at the airport took an hour because the porters were on an unannounced strike, and you missed your connection. You're dog tired; you just want to get to your room and bathe. But the receptionist at the hotel is not being particularly helpful. For starters, he or she ignored your presence for five full minutes while he or she continued a phone conversation with someone named Nicole.

Now you finally have his or her attention, and want to check into your room. But the receptionist is refusing to honor your demand because, as they point out with French logic, check-in time is only at noon. To make matters worse, this representative of the French hotel industry is displaying that popular frontal uniform of the French service industry: a frowning, unfriendly face.

Here's one for starters:

> **"Vous n'allez pas bien?"**
> ("Voo nah-lay pah byen?")
> "Are you ill?"

They may get it, but if not, inevitably, they will respond:

> **"Mais si."**
> ("May see.")
> "Not at all."

That's when you let fly with:

> **"Alors, pourquoi la gueule?"**
> ("Ah-lawr, poor-kwa la guhl?")
> "So why the sour puss?"

The chances are you will still not be handed your key and will still end up sitting in the lobby till at least one P.M., but at least you will have had the last word.

Then there is the almost inevitable encounter with our cover boy, the unremittingly snooty French waiter (and/or waitress). You know, the one who ignores your presence as long as he or she can, who insists on responding in English to the menu query you made in reasonable French, or refuses to speak English even if they know it and you don't speak French; who frowns when you make a "special" request (like bread or butter) or does that French number of blowing air out of trembling lips that indicates he or she finds you and anything you say totally intolerable.

Try this one:

"Avez-vous envisagé de faire autre chose?"
("Ahvay-voo on-vizajay duh fair owtre çhoze?")
"Have you considered another profession?"

Or the variation:

"Vous n'êtes vraiment pas fait pour ce métier."
("Voo net vray-ment pah fay poor suh met-yay.")
"You are really not made for this profession."

These aren't bad either:

"Tu es chiant."

("Too ay shiyahnt.")

(Here you are using the familiar "tu," a sign of disrespect.)

"You are an incredible pain."

"Un peu de politesse, nous n'avons pas élevé les cochons ensemble."

(Uhn peh duh powlitess, noo náhv-ohn pah eh-leveh lay koshawn ehn-sembluh.")

"A little courtesy, we didn't raise pigs together."

If that doesn't get the right response try:

"Vous pouvez vous mettre le doigt dans l'oeil."

("Voo-poo-vay voo mehtreh le dwah dahn loiye.")

"You may stick your finger in your eye."

Now comes the little shopkeeper or the sales clerk at the department store, many of whom seem to have attended the same attitude training as the disagreeable waiter/waitress.

This one usually works with the sullen type:

"Un petit sourire ne ferait pas de mal."

("Uhn petee soorear nuh fehray pah duh mal.")

"A little smile wouldn't hurt."

Or if you want to turn on your heels:

> **"Vous êtes vraiment désagréable et je m'en vais ailleurs."**
> *("Vooz ett vray-mahnt dez-agray-abluh ay zhe mon vay ay-yours.")*
> "You are truly disagreeable and I am going elsewhere."

Then, as you are opening the door to exit, turn your head backward and say,

> **"Vous donnez l'impression d'être constipé!"**
> *("Voo donn-ey l'empreshyon deh-trah kan-stee-pey!")*
> "You give the impression that you are constipated!"

The repartees that refer to a waiter's professional qualities are all useful here as well.

There are numerous all-purpose French responses to insulting behavior. If someone has made a remark about your behavior, you may simply respond:

> **"Je m'en fous."**
> *("Zhuh' mahn foo.")*
> "I couldn't care less."

There are a large number of "go to" responses in France. The most useful all-around ones, in my opinion (and the least vulgar), are:

"*Allez vous faire cuire un oeuf.*"
("*Al-ay voo fair qweer un oeff.*")
"Go boil an egg." (Not bad for restaurant use)

"*Va au diable!*"
(*Vah oh di-yabluh!*")
"Go to the devil!"

"*Allez voir ailleurs si j'y suis.*"
("*Al-ay vwahr ay-yewrs see zhy swee.*")
"Go elsewhere, see if I'm there."

"*Allez vous faire voir . . .*"
("*Al-ay voo fair vwahr . . .*")
"Go see . . ." (there are numerous endings to this phrase, but all you have to say are these four words and you will be understood).

The best all-purpose direct French insult is the word *con*. Its original meaning is not polite—it refers to a primary female body part. But in France, at least, *con* has taken on a universal meaning of idiot, jerk, dumbbell, etcetera, and is widely used even in polite company.

"*Vous êtes un vrai con!*"
("*Vooz-et un vray cunn!*")

"You're a real jerk."

There are endless varieties:

"Vous-êtes un con méchant."
("Vooz-et un cunn may-shant.")
"You're a nasty jerk."

A **gros con** *(gros cunn)* is one who makes stupid mistakes—such as, almost hits you when he tries to pass your car on the highway. A **petit con** *(petee cunn)* is a small-time jerk, and can also refer to an extremely annoying child. A **pauvre con** *(pow-vreh cunn)* is a sort of a shlub, someone who simply can't improve and is to be more pitied than scorned. A **sale con** *(sal cunn)* is the most aggressive form of the animal. Use this one with extreme caution. If you do use it, and someone moves to lay a hand on you, just yell:

"Lâchez-moi!"
("Lah'-shay mwah!")
"Leave me alone!"

Finally, there are terms of untranslatable exasperation that are fail-safe:

"Oulala!"
("Oo' la-laaaa!")

And of course the classic French expletive is always at your disposal:

"MERDE!"

(*"MAIRD!"* ["air" as in "hair"])

"SHIT!"

It works every time.

❧ ❧ ❧

French Products:
To Buy or Not to Buy

How really angry at the French are you? So annoyed at their anti-American politics that you've completely stopped drinking French wine and switched to Wisconsin cheese only? So outraged at their refusal to join in the war against Saddam Hussein that you still insist on ordering "Freedom Fries" even though it's no longer chic to do so?

Some anti-French activists have suggested a massive American boycott of French products as a way of getting back at our when-we-need-you friends in France for their disloyalty, ingratitude, and overall perverse attitude toward these United States.

And no doubt, all the French rancor notwithstanding, there is still an enormous French financial investment in America; in fact, a growing number of French companies do business in the United States. Moreover, in the un-French spirit of globalization, some American companies are now even French-owned (B.F.

Goodrich, for example, belongs to the famous French tire company Michelin).

Besides, boycotts are hard to maintain, and in some people's minds, questionably effective—not to mention economically immoral.

Besides, yet another school of thought suggests that it might ultimately be better to encourage Americans to go out of their way to buy French products. The idea is simple: The more we buy from the French, the more their economy will grow, and the more solid their economy grows, the less reason they will have to be so damned insecure and envious that they feel they can only feel better by treating the United States as though we represented the world's biggest danger to peace.

Whichever philosophy appeals to you, here is a list of some French and French-owned companies that do business in America. It may not be a complete list—thanks to the French government, which keeps the list as secret as a Swiss bank account number. While researching a column for the New York *Daily News,* I recently asked Monsieur Jean-Christophe Donnelier, the director of the French embassy's New York Economic Mission, for a "comprehensive list of French companies that sell either products or services in the U.S."

One of his assistants replied claiming that no such list was "available." Instead, she shuffled me off to the French-American Chamber of Commerce, which had already claimed it also had no such list "available." With Cartesian logic, she also attached a copy of M. Donnelier's e-mail to her; it said "Forward on to the French-American Chamber of Commerce in NY. I don't trust the Daily News to use our list of affiliates."

Anyway, here's my incomplete list. *C'est à vous de choisir*—the choice to boycott or buy is strictly yours.

Air France
Air Liquide
Airbus (airplanes in commericial use)
Alcatel
Allegra (allergy medication)
AXA Advisors
Bank of the West (owned by BNP Paribas)
Beneteau (boats)
B.F. Goodrich (owned by Michelin)
BIC (razors, pens, and lighters)
Black Bush
Bollinger (champagne)
Car & Driver *magazine*
Cartier (French founded, Swiss and Luxembourg owned)
Chanel
Chivas Regal (scotch)
Christian Dior
Club Med (vacations)
Dannon (yogurt and dairy foods)
DKNY

Dom Perignon (champagne)

J.G. Durand Crystal

Elle *magazine*

Essilor Optical Products

Evian

Fina (petroleum products) and Fina Oil (billions invested in Iraqi oil fields)

First Hawaiian Bank

Givenchy

Glenlivet (scotch)

Hennessy (liquor products)

Jacobs Creek (owned by Pernod Ricard since 1989)

Jameson (whiskey)

Jerry Springer (talk show)

Krups (coffeemakers and cappuccino machines)

Lancôme

Le Creuset (cookware)

L'Oréal (health and beauty products)

Louis Vuitton

Mandrakesoft.com

Marie Claire *magazine*

Martel Cognac

Maybelline

Mephisto (shoes and clothes)

Michelin (tires and auto parts)

Mikasa (crystal and glass)

Moët (champagne)

Motel 6

MP3.com

Mumms (champagne)

New Hermes

Nexium

Nissan (majority owned by Renault)

Nivea

Perrier

Peugeot (automobiles)

Pierre Cardin

Publicis Group (including Saatchi & Saatchi Advertising)

RCA (television and electronics—owned by Thomson Electronics–France)

Red Roof Inns (owned by Accor group in France)

Renault

Road & Track *magazine*

Rolling Stone *magazine*

Roquefort cheese (all Roquefort cheese is made in France)

Rowenta (toasters, irons, coffeemakers)

Royal Canadian

Seagram's

Sierra Software & Computer Games

Smart & Final

Sofitel (hotels, owned by Accor group)

Sparkletts (water, owned by Danone)

Technicolor

T-Fal (kitchenware)

Total Gas Stations

UbiSoft (computer games)

Uniroyal (tires)

Universal Music Group

Varilix Lenses (Essilor Optical)

Veuve Clicquot Champagne

Vittel

Vivendi

Wild Turkey (bourbon)

Woman's Day *magazine*

Yoplait (the French company Sodiaal owns a 50 percent stake)

Yves Rocher

Zodiac inflatable boats

INDEX